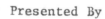

Boulevard des Misères

Boulevard des Misères

THE STORY OF
TRANSIT CAMP WESTERBORK

Jacob Boas

Archon Books • 1985

Printed in the United States of America

The paper in this book meets the guidelines for
permanence and durability of the Committee on
Production Guidelines for Book Longevity of the
Council of Library Resources.

Library of Congress Cataloging in Publication Data

Boas, Jacob.
Boulevard des Misères.

Bibliography: p.
Includes index.
1. Westerbork (Netherlands : Concentration camp)
2. Holocaust, Jewish (1939-1945)—Netherlands.
3. Jews—Netherlands—Persecutions.
4. Netherlands—
Ethnic relations. I. Title.
D805.N4B63   1985   940.53′15′039240492   85-1435
ISBN 0-208-01977-4

To
Erica, Naomi, and Demian

Men dogged our steps
So that we could not walk in our streets;
our end drew near; our days were
numbered;
for our end had come.

Lamentations of Jeremiah (4:18)

Inscription on Westerbork memorial

Contents

Acknowledgments

I wish to thank the following individuals and institutions for their assistance in the preparation of this book. The Memorial Foundation for Jewish Culture in New York for financing the initial research; the Rijksinstituut voor Oorlogsdocumentatie in Amsterdam for permission to use their archives and photographs; the Film Museum in Overveen for a private showing of the film *Westerbork,* produced by Westerbork Commandant Albert Konrad Gemmeker; Peter Davies and Ronald Rupp for their unflagging efforts in locating and sending research materials from Holland; Steven Weaver for reproducing photographs from the Rijksinstituut; and Pat, my wife, who helped with the typing and editing.

I owe a special dept of gratitude to my brother, Max. We had planned to do this book together (Westerbork was part of our earliest contacts with the world); but about one-third into *Boulevard,* other commitments put a stop to his involvement. Hence "acknowledgment" is far too narrow a term to describe his contribution.

Introduction

The film begins with a shot of a moving freight train leaving the main line. At the crossover stands a sign with the inscription "Lager Westerbork." The scene shifts to the Orange Canal, on which a ship is slowly moving towards a dock. This dock also has a sign pointing in the direction of Camp Westerbork. Shift to the main road, Hooghalen-Rolde. A moving truck; after several meters, it turns off towards Camp Westerbork. At the turn-off another sign with "Lager Westerbork."

From the script of the film *Westerbork*

What took place in Auschwitz, Sobibor, Treblinka, Maijdanek, Chelmno, and scores of other places like them, the world has long since known. But in conjunction with these dark planets, smaller satellites existed that were interdependent with the murderous system. They were found in all the German-occupied countries of Western Europe known by such names as Drancy in France, Malines in Belgium, Fossoli di Carpi in Italy, or Berg in Norway. In the scheme of annihilation they were not concentration camps, but *Durchgangslager,* transit camps.

One such, Westerbork, was in Holland. Barely a hamlet, it could be found at a tiny railway spur in Drente, a province of gloomy moors and peat bogs in the country's inhospitable northeast.

Westerbork was situated on a rude plain, broiling in summer and freezing in winter, plagued by sand, storm, and flies. Within its confines of one-half square kilometer, the inmate did not faint under punishing labor or the pangs of starvation. He did not see chimneys eject the smoke of burning flesh. In Westerbork there were no gas chambers. No graves of the massacred lay beneath its soil. There were no doctors conducting experiments on the living, nor would the inmate be suddenly struck by club or bullet.

By Nazi standards Westerbork was "humane." It was a warehouse whose inventory consisted of Jews. This material was not to be physically damaged. That, properly, was the task of the extermination camps.

At Westerbork each week a knife sliced through the inventory. Ruthlessly it lunged into the human aggregate and cut out a portion. That knife was the train. Each week it transported a thousand or more men, women, and children to Poland.

Whether the inmate stayed in Westerbork for as little as a few hours or for as long as a few years, inevitably the knife would uproot him. From the moment he entered the camp he was enrolled in the hecatombs of the Reich. Approximately 104,000 of Holland's 140,000 Jews passed through Westerbork. At the war's end, swallowed in sudden quiet, a total of 909 survivors was discovered, of whom 500 had been interned after September, 1944, when all trains to Eastern Europe had ceased.

In all, no more than 400 of those brought to Westerbork had been able to avoid deportation.

Hannah Arendt has called the destruction of Dutch Jewry "a catastrophe unparallelled in any Western country," a disaster comparable only to the extinction of Polish Jewry.

From the very beginning, before the outbreak of the war and Hitler's invasion, Westerbork seemed to have been consecrated to Dutch Jewry's calamitous end. Jews paid for Westerbork; they built it, lived there, and there they were consigned to death.

The first Jews came to Westerbork in the fall of 1939. A newspaper account of that time remarked it as a "city in the making." Oddly, the newspaper designated as "pioneers" what in reality hardly were intrepid breakers of ground. The laborers erecting the simple wooden structures were Jewish refugees from Hitler's Germany. They made up a trickle of the stream that had been washing against European borders since Germany's introduction of the Aryan edicts. Being penniless and without papers in Holland, as elsewhere, they had found themselves unwanted. The Dutch government, contending with the Depression and fearful of offending the Nazi regime, refused to grant permanent asylum, interning them instead in the limbo of Holland's poorest and least populated province. In Drente the fugitives might sit at the gate of the camp until some other countries would be found willing to admit them. There were, however, no such countries.

Under its official title—"Central Camp for Refugees, Westerbork"—the Dutch authorities had elaborated a plan to house 3,000 in some 200 small interconnected cottages and several large barracks. The tiny cottages were for families, the barracks for single men and women. The accommodations were elementary but sufficient. Each cottage contained two small rooms, a toilet, an electric hot plate, and a furzy outdoor fringe designed as a yard. The barracks were oblong shelters, about eighty-five meters in length, ten meters wide, and five-to-six meters high, with a latrine for each of the sexes.

The compound was by no means inconsiderable. But in its seclusion, in the dust that gusted up from the gorse, under the low sullen sky that seemed almost to crush the earth, Westerbork already at its incipience had the aspect of being forgotten by the world.

Westerbork's official transfer from Dutch to German hands took place on July 1, 1942. Renamed "Police Transit Camp Westerbork," the dust-choked hamlet formally entered upon its last phase as a storehouse for Jews to be "resettled" in the East.

Within a few days of the transfer the compound was visited by the Higher SS and Police Leader Hans Rauter, the general commissioner in charge of security and police matters for Holland. Immediately thereafter a two-meter-high fence sprouted on Westerbork's circumference. Seven watchtowers burgeoned at the same time, and a battalion of Dutch police arrived to ring the camp's perimeter.

But the most far-reaching transformation took place inside Westerbork, for suddenly the "pioneers"—the *Alte Kampinsassen*, or Long-Term Residents, as they had come to be known—suddenly the forgotten castaways found themselves elevated to proconsular status, with delegated power over life and death. On account of their affinities in language and culture with Westerbork's German masters, they were given every important post in the camp administration. A high proportion of them was exempted from immediate deportation—an inestimable benefit to the Jew in wartime Holland, for which wealthy Dutch Jews were willing to pay fortunes.

After having gnawed for three years the bitter root of humiliation, the German Jews took to their new power with great enthusiasm. Their authority was manifold; every aspect of camp life became subject to their control. One privilege in particular—control over the weekly "transport list"—allowed them to pronounce judgment with all the sway of the deity. While Westerbork's Commandant set the figure to be embarked on each train, a few Long-Term Residents decided who was to be included in that mortal number.

Consequently, the Dutch Jews, whom the refugees believed to have been indifferent to their previous lot, felt the weight of an oppressive arrogance on which nevertheless they depended for their lives. It was no wonder that they came to regard the German Jews as fiends, though if the full measure of their hostility were to be reckoned, an equal place would have to be allotted to their own countrymen who served on the Jewish Council.

While the German Jews processed the fate of Dutch Jews inside Westerbork, the Jewish Council handed them up before they came to the camp. Patterned after the model perfected in Vienna and Prague, the headquarters of the Jewish Council in Amsterdam was made responsible by the Germans for the collecting, assembling, and eventual transport of community members to the depot in Holland's northeast. With their scrupulous tendering of names on their registration rolls, the Council served the Germans with an alacrity that in Amsterdam complemented the expeditious work of the German-Jewish administrators in Westerbork. Virtually the entire Jewish removal from Holland was in Jewish hands.

In the unsavory history of the Jewish Councils in German-occupied Europe, none was more supine than that of Holland. In France the Jews practically ignored the Nazi-appointed body created for their delivery; in Belgium the Jewish Council succeeded in partly destroying the registration rolls; but in Holland the organization worked with all the zeal of a rampant bureaucracy, whose only desire was to preserve its own members from deportation. Nothing was too dishonorable if it answered this purpose, the most revolting instance of which was the Jewish Council's participation in the sterilization of Jews married to Aryans, a Nazi program which the Council actually subsidized.

Staffed almost exclusively by members of the middle and professional classes (its heads were a diamond merchant and a professor), the Jewish Council believed itself appointed to save the "valuable" material among Dutch Jewry. Inscribing themselves foremost in this classification, they dispatched to Westerbork the mass of poor, uneducated, and working-class Jews. The summoned who appeared before them in confusion and dismay were advised to be on time at the station for the train to Westerbork. Those who debated if they should obey the summons were threatened with severe reprisals from the Germans.

One who observed the mass of new arrivals in Westerbork was a baggage handler of the camp's "Flying Column." We do not know his name. His diary, found in the camp, asks in consternation: "Why are the members of the Jewish Council too craven to tell the truth? Why are they consistently deceiving these poor people?"

But just as the majority of Long-Term Residents in Westerbork could not avoid their fate, so the members of the Jewish Council were discarded the moment they were no longer of use to the Germans. A bitter scene took place one day at Westerbork's railway platform when a large group of neatly-dressed people was suddenly seen to disembark. Some were smoking pipes and holding briefcases. They were members of the Jewish Council. Having been abruptly ordered deported by the Nazis, they were greeted by the inmates with shouts of joy, a sickening display of grotesque, unholy glee.

The extraordinary collaboration of the Jewish leadership in Holland cannot be seen in isolation from the rest of the country. What has been called "administrative cooperation" with the Germans on the part of the Dutch was extensive. The Dutch banks played their role in the "Aryanization" of Jewish businesses, as did the Dutch civil service, the policemen of the Dutch SS, and the Dutch railways. Respectively these agencies helped expropriate, register, collect, and transport the Jewish citizens.

This easy compliance came after a brief period of open resistance, at the time—early 1941—the boldest defiance anywhere in German-occupied territories. But the series of strikes in sympathy with Jews, being organized by left-wing workers, were quickly crushed and on the whole had little following. What honor there is in the Dutch wartime record belongs to the individual citizens who at the risk of their lives concealed some fifteen thousand Jews, though not always without the inducement of money.

The ordinary Dutch Jew, hedged round by the German gun, a collaborative Dutch officialdom, and the zeal of the Jewish administrators, confronted a situation that was absolutely hopeless. Moreover, Holland, as has been noted, "was the one territory of the occupied West in which the Jews did not have an even chance to live." From Belgium about one-third fled to France; from Denmark and Norway the majority managed to cross over to Sweden. But from the small Dutch nation, with its flat, almost unwooded countryside locked in by the Reich itself, the German-occupied territories to the south, and the sea to the north and west, escape to neutral sanctuaries was virtually impossible.

Just as injurious was the thorough German political control. This alone almost completely scotched chances for survival. Shortly after the Wehrmacht invasion on May 10, 1940, Queen Wilhelmina and the entire Dutch government had fled to England, leaving the nation to a German civilian administration under a *Reichskommissar,* the Austrian jurist Seyss-Inquart. Unlike Belgium or France, which had a German military government, Holland, under German civilian rule, was treated as a protectorate, a non-incorporated territory of the Reich. Thus the SS had a free hand in implementing the Nuremberg Laws, and it was with this unhampered opportunity in mind that as early as 1941, Holland figured in Berlin as the model for the Final Solution in all European states.

The paradigm role for which the Dutch Jews had been selected in the Nazi plan of destruction was a possibility that could not have been imagined by the most pessimistic. The first tidings of German victory had struck a lighting panic into a small number of Dutch Jews. Recognizing that they were to share the treatment previously meted out to Jews in Germany, some took their lives within days of Holland's surrender. Thousands fled across the southern border, while others sought safety on the coast in hope of crossing the Channel. But the vast majority was sustained by optimism, a fatal delusion fostered by the relative temperance of the first few months of Nazi rule.

Having caught their victim in a trap, the Germans could afford to play the game at leisure. More than two years elapsed before the first train departed from Westerbork. In the meantime the Dutch Jews had been gradually excluded from civil life. As early as July, 1940, they had been dismissed from the Dutch press, forbidden to practice ritual slaughter, and barred from joining their Dutch neighbors in civil defense maneuvers. In all these curtailments the terrible optimism did not forsake the victims. Comparing their treatment to the earlier Jewish persecution in Germany, they almost congratulated themselves on being accorded greater circumspection.

Holland's long-standing reputation for tolerance led the

Germans to proceed gradually, a policy that prevailed until early 1941. By that time authority over Jewish affairs in Berlin had been vested in the Jewish Department of Heydrich's Security Service, Section IVB4, which a year later was to be headed by Adolf Eichmann. A branch of IVB4, the Central Office for Jewish Emigration, began operating in Holland in September, 1941, under the infamous Austrian, Ferdinand Aus der Fünten.

Again, the effects were not immediately apparent, the most severe being the transport of several hundred young Jewish men who had been made to pay the price of a series of "attacks" on Nazis in the Jewish quarter by being sent to Mauthausen, the stone quarrying camp in Austria, where they quickly perished under torture. But the final repressive measures did not commence until the spring of 1942, when a whirlwind of orders and decrees cast up the victims like straw before reducing them to dust.

On July 15, 1942, when Westerbork's population had doubled to nearly 1,400 people—mostly, at this early stage, still German Jews—the first transport stopped at a siding near the camp. The train had originated in Amsterdam, and it halted at Westerbork to take on board 175 inmates to "fill out" the shipment. From then on the work of human destruction proceeded rapidly. Within a year and a half the Jews vanished from the Dutch soil on which they had lived for centuries.

Westerbork offered Dutch Jews the last contact with their native ground, and a history of human despair might be written merely from the catalogue of hopes, efforts, and ruses that were employed by the inmates in trying to stay in the camp. Though the victims had no certain knowledge of their allotted end, believing by and large they were being recruited to work for the German war machine, they shared the intuitive foreboding of the doomed. In Poland they sensed their extinction.

All the more strenuous, therefore, were the energies of will and ingenuity the inmates applied to keeping off the weekly, and sometimes twice-weekly, transport list. For those who succeeded in prolonging their stay in Westerbork, the camp was not intolerable. Within its perimeter was relief from the German persecution in the rest of Holland. In the transit camp, from the policeman on his beat to the chief administrator, Jews were in authority. Westerbork's Potemkin-like aspect with its facsimiles of "normal" community life beguiled the inmate. There were even times when he felt himself a pampered guest, subject to the most solicitous care.

But we who know how vain were the hopes of the doomed, how pathetic their wiles, we may be able to see Westerbork without false coloring. In fact, Westerbork, mired in squalor and wretchedness, with its ramshackle barracks bursting with people and its air tremulous with unrest, was a gruesome place. The name given to its one paved road and main street contained the full horror that infested the camp. Traversing Westerbork and running alongside the railway platform, it was called Boulevard des Misères. Boulevard des Misères was also the last plot of Dutch ground the feet of Jews touched before they boarded the train.

If Westerbork had an atmosphere, it was that which arose from the inhuman grating of nerves stretched by the will to live. While outwardly life seemed bearable, each inmate was an Atlas shouldering a world of apprehension. The fear of the transports that would take them to the unknown, the intimations of extinction at the end of the line, the unreality of adhering to a normal life in an abnormal setting, all these made existence in Westerbork perhaps more harrowing psychologically than that in the actual death camps of Poland, where the executioner had doffed his mask, and illusion was no longer.

1

Konrad

COMMANDANT

*The truck arrives at the turnpike. Stop.
Inspection. The driver shows a paper to the
guard on duty: a permit to enter the camp,
written on official stationery, signed by the*
Obersturmführer. *Close-up of the signature.
Fade out . . . .*

*The permit lies on the desk in the office of the
camp commandant. Shot of the*
Obersturmführer; *of a photograph of the*
Führer, *and so forth . . . . Commandant leaves
office to go on inspection tour of the camp, after
being helped with his coat, hat and gloves by a
subordinate whom he has summoned with a bell
. . . . Shot of the Camp High Command.*

From the film script of *Westerbork*

In January, 1949, at the Park Hotel in the Dutch city of Assen, Albert Konrad Gemmeker, the former Commandant of Westerbork, appeared before the Special Court dealing with war criminals. Those in the court room who knew him only as the officer who had sent 80,000 Jews to their deaths were astonished. The spectators had expected to see a primeval type, a bruiser with a blockbuster jaw, "a low forehead, blinking eyelids and prominent cheekbones." Instead they discovered a man who could easily have passed for the secretary at a foreign legation.

The years of confinement since the war's end had failed to deprive him of a certain élan. Gemmeker stood before the judge completely self-possessed. He was sprucely tailored, smoothly shaven, faultlessly trim. His voice and gestures had a compelling precision.

"You had no objection," he was asked by the president of the court, "that the Jews were being interned and deported in this way?"

"*Nein.*"

"And why did you have no objection? What was your standpoint?"

"*Ich hatte die Auffassung*—I was of the opinion, after what I had heard and learned about these matters in Germany, and what I had been told about the First World War, that it would be necessary to intern this group of people during the war."

"For military reasons?"

"On military and political grounds."

"If that is so, how do you explain that among these dangerous people who had to be interned there were very elderly as well as very young people. There were eighty-year-old women and two-year-old children. How can you justify this on military and political grounds?"

"The question can be answered as follows: that the Reich government wished to deal with this problem by gathering up the group as a whole, including the families, so that they could stay together as it was done by me at Westerbork."

The president wanted to know about the transports. Weren't the conditions under which the prisoner shipped people to the East inhuman?

"I admit only that the transport of these individuals in freight cars was inhuman. The people were stuffed inside because no more room had been allocated and the transports had to be carried out to the letter. The railway people continually informed me that the conditions under which our soldiers, and even the wounded, were being transported, were not any better."

The defendant answered with an ease that was highly persuasive. Everyone was impressed with his civilized appearance. He spoke quietly and stood straight up. The spectators who had come to revile, insensibly were being confirmed in his favor.

On the bench, too, all was respectful, low-key, very proper, *zakelijk*, very Dutch.

And what did the accused know about Auschwitz?

"However improbable it may sound to you, I did not know what would happen to the Jews in Auschwitz."

Did he have any knowledge of the deaths of the approximately one hundred thousand Dutchmen who had been sent from Westerbork?

"That became known to me after the war during my interrogation."

Did he know about the gas chambers?

"*Nein, es wurde ganz allgemein im Lager behauptet*—No, it was generally believed in the camp that people were dying there, and I asked the Hague about that. They said these were rumors."

Nor, he said, was this the only time he had checked with headquarters. On one such occasion, his superiors had told him that thousands of Jews were being sent to Riga to work for the German military in clothing, leather, and synthetic rubber factories. In addition, he said, he had questioned a former Auschwitz official about the fate of the Jews there, and this man had reassured him that many of them were being used in the demolition of downed airplanes. "All this information reinforced what I had been told by the Hague—that death was altogether out of the question; that these were rumors—so that I had no grounds for believing otherwise."

Citing the testimony of Nico Speijer, a Jewish doctor in

14

Westerbork, the president asked whether the defendant could remember ever having said, "The ovens of the camp at Auschwitz are going full blast."

He was not sure. So much had happened, so much he could not "remember exactly." But if he had, it could only have been in connection with the industry he knew to exist at Auschwitz.

The president asked whether the accused had experienced any problems with his conscience.

"*Nein, Herr Richter*—No, your honor. I must say that after I saw how things were in Westerbork, through personal observation, that *there* I did experience a strong conflict of conscience. But I was not in the position to articulate it to higher authorities and express criticism. There then was only one thing left: to do whatever lay in my power to salvage from the situation what I could by making it as tolerable as possible."

So you would have liked it best if everything had gone in a pleasant manner."

"I came to the conclusion that internment in a camp—like Westerbork, or such—should be the worst that should happen to the inmates. And that later they should be able to come back to their country or be settled in Palestine."

Before the accused came to Westerbork, he had no previous experience with Jews. Until Adolf Hitler took power the city of Düsseldorf, where Gemmeker grew up, had not been a stronghold of antisemitism. He had learned antisemitism from "Party politics." He had learned that Jews, as parasites and exploiters, were responsible for Germany's defeat in World War I. He had come to see, through Party lectures and literature, that Jews dominated the German press, culture, and economy. The necessity of expelling Jews from these areas had become clear to him.

"And how were they to be ousted from that position?"

"By fair means," replied Gemmeker.

"And what would happen to them afterwards?"

Originally, the defendant stated, the Jews were to have been given the opportunity to leave Germany, with Palestine as the preferred location for their resettlement. But with the outbreak of the war the policy changed, and the Jewish question became a military problem of international proportions whose resolution was crucial to victory. After the war, after Hitler had won, Germany would honor its prewar pledge and send the Jews to Palestine. Meanwhile, to prevent them from "stabbing Germany in the back," as in 1918, they had been interned in camps. This had the sanction of international law. In no way was it "in conflict with the laws and customs of humanity."

The president pointed out that under German military law an officer or a soldier could refuse orders that blatantly violated the code governing the conduct of war, and that his superior, Dr. Harster, had testified that the accused had never petitioned him to be relieved on that basis.

Gemmeker said his conscience was clear: *"Von mir aus habe ich nichts getan—I did nothing on my own. . . ."*

Albert Konrad Gemmeker was born in 1907, in Düsseldorf, the chief city of the industrial Rhineland. He had no family of name, connections, or wealth. He could boast no history or illustrious ancestors. His family had become impoverished during the Depression, sinking to the lower middle class. In this sphere a grim economy reigned, and at fourteen his school days were over. He made his submission to life by entering an insurance firm, where six years later he was established as a salesman.

At twenty he made a momentous decision. The steady application to his paper-and-pencil work had satisfied his superiors; he had been promoted to salesman. But barely had he settled in his new job, when he left. The prospect of conjuring calamities to hesitant buyers apparently did not agree with him.

Unfortunately, having neither education nor acquaintances with influence to appoint him a berth, he was not fit for much. And so he looked to the only avenue open to the anonymous— the civil service, the mammoth institution of German life that met the average citizen's passion for paperwork, authority, and respect. In 1927 Konrad Gemmeker enrolled in the Police Academy at Bonn where for a year he studied police administration. Graduating with the rank of sergeant, he joined the municipal police force in Duisburg, about twenty-five kilometers from Düsseldorf. In 1933 he returned to his hometown to take a job with the local police force as chief sergeant, serving in an administrative capacity.

It was while Gemmeker was still working as police clerk in Duisburg that Hitler scored his election victory. So electrified was the young man by this news that within days of the Nazi triumph he applied for membership in the National Socialist Party, though up till then his enthusiasm for Hitler had not been much in evidence. But under the new leadership an expansion of police work was foreseen, and in such an atmosphere being a card-carrying police official could only be favorable. The Nazi Party, however, in the full flush of its supremacy, had developed a jealous suspicion of those it called "January National Socialists," people who had discovered their Nazi convictions on the day Hitler became chancellor. There was a flood of these in the first months of 1933. The Führer's veterans anxiously searched for taints of opportunism in the sudden throng of applicants like the police clerk at Duisburg.

While waiting to be accepted, Gemmeker in 1935 managed to obtain a minor position with the Gestapo. With this job he hoped to prove himself, his loyalty and worth. Since there had been friction between Hitler and the Vatican, he supposed he might further his chances by leaving the church into which he had been born. And in 1937, after having waited four years, he became a Party member. Immediately upon his enrollment he was made Police Secretary, as well as *Blockleiter*, the lowly Nazi official who informed on the politics of fifty households.

In the same year he applied for membership in the SS, and in 1940 was accepted into Hitler's elite guard. The outbreak of the war continued to give impetus to his career; first with his promotion to *Obersturmführer* (Lieutenant), and later with his being awarded the War Merit Cross Without Swords, the Nazi decoration for meritorious service of a nonmilitary nature.

In August, 1940, a few months after the German invasion of Holland, Gemmeker appeared in the Hague to assume a desk job in the personnel department of the Commander of the Security Police and Security Service, Dr. W. Harster, the representative of Heydrich's German State Security Service. Harster was ultimately responsible for the transport of Jews from Holland. His deputy was Willi Zöpf who took his orders directly from Eichmann, and it was Zöpf whose increasing partiality for the unassuming administrator in the personnel office propelled his advancement. For Gemmeker had that singular talent of mediocrity: he was able to please his superiors.

For nearly two years he clung to a dull job. Though his work hardly drew on his police experience, he did not murmur. Wisely he stayed away from squabbles. Ever dutiful, he contrived, by a formal cordiality, to avert the envy of his colleagues.

With his new duties and rank, Gemmeker's early restlessness was appeased; all the insecurities of the insurance clerk had become inert, secured by the insignia of the SS. There was about him now an absolute stability. He wore the mask of callous indifference. He had become "correct." He was, in the words of survivors, "ice-cold."

In June, 1942, Gemmeker received his first promotion. He was put in charge of an internment camp for hostages in southern Holland. As this was his first experience in command, a vestigial timidity did not go unnoticed by the inmates. But this trace of clerkish character was to be submerged when several months later he received his appointment to Westerbork. The full accoutrement of the SS persona was to be paraded without a flaw before the captives of the transit camp.

Gemmeker's elevation came at a time when the railroads of Europe had been converted into one bloody armature, the great mass deportation of Jews from Western Europe having begun in mid-1942. In Poland and Russia, where the Germans had never felt compelled to observe delicacies, the reduction of Jews through starvation and mass executions had continued apace for two years. But the more methodical annihilation of Western European Jews had to await the completion of the giant death camp at Auschwitz, the final destiny of most Dutch Jews, which began consuming its human fuel in the spring of 1942.

Just days before Gemmeker took up his new duties, the order had been given from Berlin to "clear out" the concentration camps in preparation for the influx of fresh victims. Coinciding with this stepped-up pace of destruction was the decree in Holland proscribing Jews. Since the previous May, they had been compelled to wear the distinctive star, and the new ruling in effect made Dutch Jews outlaws, who by virtue of their visible symbol, could be arrested at will.

Until this decree, the deportations from Holland had been sporadic. The worst had been two punitive transports to Mauthausen, while the program as a whole had remained fraught with difficulties, exemptions, evasions, and often contradictory directions from Berlin. The ruthless dispatch with which the Germans proceeded to implement the new orders was noticeable in Amsterdam, where by April, 1943, almost no Jews were left.

Gemmeker's installation at Westerbork resulted from the necessary efficiency with which the camp was to be operated in view of the increased transports. Since the previous July, when the Germans had taken over Westerbork from the Dutch, the camp had gone through three Commandants. The first had been a degenerate, the second a whip-wielding alcoholic, the third an abysmal cipher. Together they had managed to ship off 23,000 Jews, though under tumult and disorder.

Under the new Commandant an additional 80,000 would vanish. But noiselessly, impalpably, as if the air had dissolved them.

In the second week of October, 1942, the prisoners of Westerbork noticed a tall, taciturn SS officer stalking the camp. He was as indefatigable as a tourist. He paced about all day. His curiosity never ceased. At night he disappeared, with his dog frisking about his legs. He was lodging in the villa just outside the camp's perimeter.

But the next day he returned. Again, in the alleys between the barracks, his leathern tread was heard. The inmates saw him pop up here, then there. The light green cap with the morbid insignia was seen poking into the kitchen. Next it turned its brim into the laundry room. The barbed wire and watchtowers received critical attention. And, coldly and aloof, the man would study them, the "transport material." By nightfall he had vanished once more in the direction of the villa.

Not until a few days later did the inmates learn that the silent, briskly pacing visitor was their new Commandant.

Gemmeker's dramatic entry was the beginning of a fascination among the captives that would last not only for the duration of the camp, but even beyond. For long after the war, and even to this day, not a few survivors would speak of "their Commandant" in genteel terms.

One such was a German Jew, Kurt Schlesinger. As the camp's Chief Administrator, Schlesinger was responsible, among other things, for compiling the transport lists, a task which required him to work at close quarters with the *Obersturmführer*. Called as a witness in the proceedings against the Commandant, and recalling the two and a half years his former master ruled the moor, Schlesinger testified that "Gemmeker was a good commandant, who prized order, calm, and humanity." That was not just his opinion, he added, but one shared by the "inmate population in general" whom he impressed with "his camouflaged sense of justice." "I for one," Schlesinger averred, "was never under the impression that Gemmeker personally would have taken the initiative to deport people."

As Westerbork was being constantly depopulated by trains going East and replenished by trains from Amsterdam and the provinces, the legend of the Commandant's beneficence spanned the dozens of brief camp generations. Each inmate would quickly learn that Gemmeker was "charming" and "humane"; that he was a "gentleman"; that he was "fair"; that he appeared to have been "decently brought up." Some even pronounced him "well disposed towards Jews." And even the more skeptical went no further than to appraise him an "enigma," someone they had not yet been quite able to fathom.

These sentiments passed current by inmates whom each week the Commandant drove into cattle cars for a journey to their end. The same people who praised his "humaneness" could see him stride past the wagons bursting with men, women, and children, many of them ill and dumped any which way from stretchers. Those who thought him "well disposed towards Jews" watched him march past the train like a general inspecting a routed band—the wretched troops of Westerbork loaded with bags and blankets: the young mothers and their infants, the hale youths and bent ancients, the young girls and boys, and the pied patches among the human mass, the shaven heads of the punishment cases. The legend was still very much alive in September, 1944, when with German defeat virtually assured, Gemmeker made a final sweep of his desk, sending off Holland's last victims to Bergen-Belsen.

Westerbork's strange infatuation can only be understood in the light of its single all-pervasive reality: fear. Fear was everywhere, touching all. And being of all the emotions the most distorting, it warped the perceptions of all but a few inmates. In their Commandant the prisoners saw "correctness." In their lamentable anxiety that "correctness" became "humane." They rarely heard him raise his voice. Thus he became a "gentleman." Gemmeker did not boot them off to Poland, as one inmate wryly remarked; he sent them off with a smile. Therefore, they thought him "fair."

To the powerless the least caprice of the master takes on a grandiose significance. At Westerbork Gemmeker was the master of subjects whose future subsisted as a profound darkness in which he glowed as the only light to what might be awaiting them. Westerbork had reduced the Jews to helots, and in weighing the actions of their master they translated his whims into the hope of a merciful future. That Gemmeker served as a forwarding agent of death they could neither know nor would have believed. They invested him with their optimism, which is the allopathy of fear.

Instances to inspire them were never lacking. Reassurance came to Westerbork when it heard that Gemmeker had laughed heartily at the camp cabaret. His solicitude for their diet was acclaimed when he ordered marrow peas to be substituted for cabbage. Happy was the knowledge of his fondness for children, to the extent, exuded the enthusiasts, that in the camp hospital the tots were to be given a daily tomato. So pathetic was the inmates' despair that a jubilant rumor might be founded on nothing more than the sight of Gemmeker taking a different road from the Commandant of Vught during a visit by that officer. At Vught, the labor camp in the south of Holland, conditions were notorious, and it was the prisoners' consensus that "their Commandant" was incensed with his colleague over the recent transport he had sent to Westerbork, which had consisted of prisoners in rags and bearing the unmistakable signs of vicious abuse. By such propitious interpretations were fears appeased and the Commandant's "humanity" ordained.

But a few of the captivity beheld him with unclouded vision. In Westerbork there were a man and a woman who were haunted by what they saw and felt. A compulsion to bear witness drove them to register their impressions. They noted the life of the camp and shared the general fascination with the Commandant. Stealthily, sometimes through the crack of a barrack door, or unnoticed from a distance, they studied the clerk who ruled life and death on the heath.

For weeks and months during 1943 and part of 1944 the camp's life was recorded by Philip Mechanicus. He roamed the camp and after his rounds he stole away to pour his heart into a diary.* Mechanicus had done extensive reading and he had traveled widely. As a reporter and author, who had written books about Palestine and the Soviet Union, his experience had covered a broad range. But it seemed that in Gemmeker he had come upon a creature utterly foreign. The diarist was hard put to detect in him the human affections. Gemmeker provoked him as a moral quandary. Almost obsessively he combed him for a recognizable human strand. He examined him like a patient for symptoms of honest emotion, sympathy, or passion. At last, in dismay, he was forced to conclude his case, noting, "You cannot see the workings of his heart."

In his diary, Mechanicus mentions talking on the night before a transport to a woman "with a clear, perceptive mind" whose name was Esther, "Etty," Hillesum, a twenty-nine-year-old doctor of jurisprudence. As an employee of the Jewish Council with visiting privileges at Westerbork, she wrote from the camp two lengthy letters, which were subsequently published in the wartime underground press—letters of extraordinary power and singular purity.

Esther Hillesum's observations on Gemmeker were characteristically wry and detached. He intrigued her, but by seeing in

---

*Unless indicated otherwise, all translations from Mechanicus' diary are from the English translation by Irene S. Gibson, *Year of Fear: A Jewish Prisoner Waits for Auschwitz* (New York: 1968).

him something of the strutting martinet she was also able to be amused. Mechanicus, too, could be sarcastic about the Commandant, but more so was he baffled. While the diarist looked at the Commandant with the masculine eye, Esther Hillesum sized him up with direct female penetration. She saw that in Gemmeker's physical appearance lay the camp's unreasoning prepossession.

At the time of his Westerbork appointment, Gemmeker was thirty-five years old. He was tall, almost ascetically gaunt, with a still youthful face in which the features were so evenly formed and so happily distributed as to seem rather chiseled. Nevertheless, this attenuated regularity would have been unexceptional if not for one striking variation. That was his hair. Unseasonably, for his years, it was gray. The silvery fringe, always exquisitely brushed, lent an unusual contrast to the Commandant's composition. And the adornment of a flat green cap completed the mood of a romantic mezzotint. Not a few of the women inmates fell under this spell. Innocent teenagers secretly entertained a "crush on that gray hair." They saw a "handsome German officer," in whose facial landscape the harpy pitch of the train melted and the dispatcher of death faded and became an erotic symbol.

Gemmeker projected the perfection of the idealized Aryan, that is, a physical "correctness." His fabled "charm" described in very detail the racial prototype Heinrich Himmler, the Reich Security Chief, favored for his SS. But as beauty without spirit and intelligence is the beauty of a mask, Esther Hillesum found him odious. His face repelled her. She thought it resembled "a small scar in which grimness, joylessness, and insincerity had fused together to form a whole."

For nigh two years the Commandant ruled the moor in serenity. The war during all that time made little impact on his domain. A slow strangulation between the hosts of the East and West had seized the Reich. But for long hardly a sigh was heard in the forgotten corner of Drente. Everything there took its regular course. The purple lupin bloomed in summer, in winter blew a biting wind, the dust never ceased to contrive fabulous clouds. Routinely Gemmeker authorized the transports. Routinely departed the trains. And routinely the inmates died.

It was in this terrible abode, with its imperturbable function, that the former clerk was able to act out his great fantasy. Like most people's it was the fantasy of power. To play the part, he endowed the incredible role of Commandant. He wore a moss-green uniform and top boots. At his hip was a gun, in his gloved hands a crop. At his heels grazed a hound, and where he strode the mass of humanity trembled.

The quality of theater being inseparable from the exercise of power, Gemmeker lived his drama intensely. As backstage rumbled the great war and from the wings streamed the moribund, he stood at center stage, giving countenance to the few who might live, attesting his indifference to the many who would perish. He gave orders curtly. All his attitudes evinced severe control. But most often, on the camp's squalid boards, he did nothing save silently strut.

In this drama he had but to appear to create tremendous suspense. And never was this quality greater than when the train, amidst the bedlam of tears and farewells, stood panting by the platform. While the terror-stricken populace by shoves and shouts of the camp police was being forced into the wagons, he would survey them regally with self-possessed, superior aplomb. He had delayed to appear, as if to tantalize with his absence, until just before curtain time.

The fantasy and the power mutually embraced in Gemmeker's personal establishment. Just outside the camp stood his villa, a compact latifundium with its own chicken farm, truck garden, and greenhouse. The glass structure had been built to order so that its temperate air might yield him the flowers of which he was fond. The exterior of the villa had a plain Dutch solidity, proclaiming not luxury but comfort, good plumbing and heating, and a plentiful board. Behind the windows' trim lace curtains were assembled the ponderous furniture and suffocating kitsch favored by the German middle class. But not a few articles among the appurtenances were of higher quality. These had been handpicked by the Commandant from the Jewish property that occasionally tumbled through the camp from Amsterdam.

A legion of slaves swarmed over his estate. They served, they labored, and performed tasks of skill. Tailors, shoemakers, furriers, and barbers attended to his person. Carpenters, repairmen, roofers, plumbers, electricians, and glaziers kept him comfortably housed. At his beck were goldsmiths, watchmakers, diamond cutters, mechanics. His food was prepared to his specification. He even numbered in his retinue a sculptor to blazon his likeness in plastic form.

The Commandant did not live alone on the heath. He shared his life with a consort who had been his secretary in the Hague when he was still an administrative clerk at the personnel desk. No two beings could have been better matched than the Commandant and Frau Elisabeth Hassel.

A commonplace woman, devoid of the least allurement, a sour scrawl was the normal expression of her long bony face. The Westerbork inmates had a saying that after the war they wished to hang Gemmeker with a velvet cord, but they reserved no such delicacy regarding the halter for Frau Hassel. She was known in the camp as a "she-devil" and a fearsome tormentor. Only at the transports was she seen to smile and laugh, never failing to attend every departure, occupying the platform as if it were the stall at a matinee from which she looked on. The inmates thought her the "evil spirit of Gemmeker," and they believed that the Commandant appeared to be more "humane" in her absence.

The Commandant had been married twice. His first marriage had ended in 1934, but while there were no children, the second produced three, with the first arriving before the connubial tie had been knotted. In 1944, after living several years with Frau Hassel, he petitioned for divorce, though by the end of the war his request was still shelved.

Frau Hassel also hailed from Düsseldorf. She was also still married, to an official with the *Sicherheitsdienst* in Amsterdam. At their trial both Gemmeker and Frau Hassel implied that each, after unhappy marriages, had found happiness on the Dutch moor. The unfortunate end of the war had not dimmed their romance. "The love relationship between myself and Gemmeker," Frau Hassel stated to the court, "has endured and still exists. We still have hopes of getting married one day."

At Westerbork the Commandant's mistress shared his dominion with all its royal amenities. Her initial appearance in the camp had shown her in frumpy attire, but she soon improved to more opulent taste. The books of the repair and tailor shops found after the war testified to the furs, dresses, and smartly fitted suits in which she chose to exhibit herself. In Westerbork she was the pharaoh's wife. In Gemmeker's absence she became absolute mistress, and at such times the inmates slunk out of her way and even SS-men cringed.

She relished her imperious role and the startling effect of an impatient or angry look. The more attractive female members of the cabaret were especially apt to experience the full force of her displeasure. They excited her to a silent fury, for this cabaret, toward which Frau Hassel manifested an undisguised aversion, fascinated her consort.

Gemmeker's attraction to the stage was unequivocal. Rarely missing a show, his absorption was complete. Esther Hillesum noted that once he came three times in succession to the same performance, and that each time he laughed at the same stale jokes. At times he even took a personal hand in staging the productions. He enjoyed playing the patron of Westerbork's cultural life. On show days his private front row seat, a plush chair, remained under the jealous protection of a Jewish servant. And never did he appear more benign than when with grateful gesture he signaled the audience, which had risen at his entrance, to be seated.

Seated on the plush chair, he reverted to the infant who reaches for toys and trinkets. In the confraternity of the theater Gemmeker so much forgot himself that he ordered the male choir to sing *Bei Mir Bist Du Schön,* a song forbidden in Germany because of its Yiddish flavor. In the same feeling of fellowship he liked to forgather, after a revue performance, with the members of the cast, to prolong the good feeling over schnapps and cigars.

His mindless amusement was part of a cheap and vulgar quality which the perceptive never failed to notice. He struck Esther Hillesum as "a cross between a well-groomed barber's assistant and the habitué of an artists' hang-out." Gemmeker also sought out Westerbork's sports people, especially its boxers, whom he would treat in exhibition to visiting officials. But the fear that his lack of schooling lay open to the view of the more educated and that his coarseness was evident to the more cultured, led him perversely to one group of inmates in particular. These were known as the *Barnevelders*, due to their having been previously interned, thanks to a special exemption, in a Dutch castle by that name. They constituted the "camp intelligentsia." Eventually they were to be sent from Holland to Theresienstadt, the "privileged" camp in Bohemia.

In Westerbork the Barnevelders were housed in a special barrack that drew the Commandant compulsively. The inmates—most of them professors, teachers, writers, and artists—became the target of his frequent and obsessive inspections. He had confiscated their books. And they had also been among the few who had seen his composure, as if giving way under strain, suffer a crack, a brief collapse.

This rare event took place during a "shoe inspection." Apparently unhappy with their polishing skills, Gemmeker had personally grabbed hold of one of the offending shoes and rubbed it with such unholy ardor that the barrack shook. Upon withdrawing the cloth the spot he had been trying to remove was still there, and Gemmeker had begun to babble excitedly, both threatening and cajoling, at last promising a voucher for a *new* pair of shoes to the flabbergasted owner.

During the whole episode he had carried on so bizzarely that Philip Mechanicus seriously wondered if the Commandant was insane. At the least, the diarist believed, that there was "definitely something wrong with him."

The scene with the Barnevelders was unusual only because of its context. Gemmeker was not unknown to lose his self-control, though commonly nothing but some outrage in connection with his trains was capable of provoking this reaction. For the train was his obsession just as much as the inmates'. Both lived in complete thrall to its appetite—Gemmeker by wishing to satisfy its voracity, the Jews by wishing to escape it.

Each week the Commandant received from the Hague a waybill for human goods to be delivered to Poland, and in filling the order lay his sole account. He rejoiced in his absolute responsibility in this regard, and any interference with the

27

transport resulted in the anxiety which fears to disappoint the trust of superiors. His only grief appeared to be that the Jews could not see it that way.

Very strangely, there had grown up in his mind a belief in some sort of compact between himself and the inmates. The relative leniency and occasional liberties he permitted were predicated on good faith on the part of the inmates in holding up their end of this unspoken agreement. By this logic the Jews owed him the courtesy of obediently boarding the trains in exchange for "just dealings" from his side. For such favors as being allowed to pick berries, for example, he expected grateful compliance at the time of deportation. Thus, when prisoners hid themselves or were found to have escaped, he was as angry as he was disappointed. A willful obstruction of the transport had been committed. The compact had been broken—and under hurt feelings and offended dignity, Gemmeker's equability collapsed.

At his trial a witness described the Commandant's fury upon learning that two inmates scheduled for transport had escaped. Gemmeker stormed into the barrack, where a section of the deportees had been put up, ". . . foaming with rage, ranting and raving, completely beside himself, cursing . . . screaming that is was 'uncomradely behavior.' " About fifty people were in the barrack at the time, S-cases (punishment cases), most of them near death and wearing next to nothing. The Commandant then proceeded personally to help "lift those people from their beds, twenty men, after which they were dragged through the cold and mud and thrown into the train a few minutes before its departure."

As time went on, and with the deteriorating war news, Gemmeker began to deal more brutally with the "ingrates." The execution of four inmates in September, 1944, was brought up at his trial. They had been caught in the act of escaping and by his orders were shot out of hand. For one who was still alive after the shooting, Gemmeker ordered a lethal injection. In reply to this accusation in the Assen courtroom, Gemmeker submitted that he had followed orders from the Security Police, reminding the judges that this was a *Kriegssituation*, a war situation, and a very critical period for Germany.

But normally, if he did not think of Barnevelders and there was no trouble with the trains, Gemmeker remained "correct." "Here we were not being kicked or beaten," stated a former inmate of Westerbork at the trial, "but the punishment was much subtler. Because for every mild transgression you were sent on transport, and that meant death."

Death by transport was Gemmeker's privilege. Though rarely taking a hand in the actual formation of the weekly transport list—this being the task of the German-Jewish camp aristocracy—he gave it the final approval and reserved the liberty to put on it whomever he pleased. Anyone who in whatever manner offended him personally would be put on the list. It happened to the gardener who failed to doff his cap to him and to the parent whose child broke a window. It happened to the young woman whom he overheard impugn Germany and to the fifty inmates of one barrack who were seized because a boy in blue pajamas hid himself in a tent in order to escape the train.

At his trial Gemmeker, quite truthfully, portrayed himself as an official devoted to his duty. The cruel dilemmas he posed to the inmates were part of that duty, he implied. In June of 1943, for instance, he gave the Jewish male partners in mixed marriages the choice of being sent to Poland where, he informed them, "they would collapse under the inhuman system of labor," or letting themselves be sterilized. Sterilized, they would be free to return to Amsterdam without a star and live with their families. Two months later, the rag sorters and furriers were given the option of either going to Vught, the concentration camp in southern Holland, or escorting their wives to the East. At one point, determined to rid the hospital of "malingerers," he told the patients that he would let them stay where they were, provided they did not mind abandoning their spouses, as he was about to deport them.

More than the countless regulations that streamed from the Commandant's office, it was his personal threat of transport that maintained the camp's astonishing order. Inmates who had kept their dogs unleashed, for instance, at once hastened to have them killed when ordered to do so on pain of deportation.

However, Gemmeker liked it best when there was no need

29

to rage or punish, when things went smoothly, the deportees without murmur packing their bags, conveying themselves along Boulevard des Misères and stuffing themselves in the cattle cars. Nothing was likely to give him greater offense than a disorderly transport. Instances were known in which, upset by the improper disposition of the train's human ballast, he would condescend to assist and with his own gloved hands push the wretched victim, some man, woman, or child, inside the packed door, like so! By contrast, never did he show greater benignity, even respect, than to the Zionist youth group as, singing and marching in close formation, the young men and women boarded the train. He was observed giving them a stern salute and heard to remark, "A people with such youth cannot perish."

For Gemmeker, observed Esther Hillesum, the Dutch camp was little more than a place where a still relatively young man might distinguish himself. He inhabited its wretched locale with one foot on the rung, the other already poised for ascent. Westerbork was a step in his career; he brought no personal animus to the Dutch Jews who comprised this step. Even though he had learned about Jews from "Party politics," he bore them no ill feelings. In his dealings with Jews he showed himself wholly free from antisemitism—he did not even refer to them as "Jews," but always as *Lagerinsassen*, "camp inmates."

Gemmeker's kindness toward Jews was one of the camp's favorite legends, instances of which were being constantly recounted. It was said that while attending a Hanukkah ceremony, he appeared to have been moved by the songs and the candles. Mechanicus in stupefaction marked in his diary Gemmeker's comment, as relayed to him by a Jewish camp leader: "I care more about the Jews than about many of my own SS men," the Commandant was supposed to have said. Gemmeker believed that he was giving Jews "the best treatment possible under National Socialism."

One day during the trial of Albert Konrad Gemmeker the courtroom darkened. On the wall behind the bench a white square appeared which rapidly filled with images and shadows.

Seventy minutes later the lights came back on. It was the end of the film *Westerbork*, produced by *Obersturmführer* Gemmeker.

The president of the court asked what the purpose of this film might have been.

"*Ich habe mit diesem Film*—With this film, which was made *for* the camp and for showing *in* the camp, I tried to record everything, including the sadder aspects, in order that it might not be said that I only focused on the better side of the camp."

Despite its poor quality and amateurishness, considerable care appeared to have gone into the production. The script was written by Gemmeker's Jewish secretary, and the crew had also consisted of inmates. Gemmeker stated that it had been shown in Westerbork, and that it had been appreciated, including, presumably, *die Traurige*, the sad parts. The scenes touching on his own person had a solitary, brooding quality.

What was remarkable, the court found, was that the film had been made on Gemmeker's own initiative. Unlike the Nazi documentaries of other camps like Auschwitz, with such scenes as Jews busily checking books out of the libarary, *Westerbork* was not a propaganda film. It had been made outside the proper Nazi channels. It had no official approval from either the Hague or Berlin.

After the war, amidst the rubble of Auschwitz, a photo album was found belonging to an SS-man filled with pictures taken in the death camp and entitled "The Best Years of My Life." It is possible that Gemmeker's film *Westerbork* was designed as a similar souvenir, to be unrolled of an evening in Düsseldorf with Frau Hassel. But a practical purpose seemed more likely. The film had been made toward mid-1944, when the tide against Germany had unalterably turned, and it had been made for none but the president of the court in Assen. On celluloid, just before the German military collapse, the Commandant had prepared his brief for the "humane" administrator who had run a "model" camp.

At his trial, Gemmeker was charged principally with having deprived Jews of their freedom "solely on account of their Jewish origin . . . deliberately and contrary to the laws and customs of war." The accused defended himself with the standard argument—*Befehl ist Befehl*, "orders are orders." But his case rested primarily on the role he had portrayed in the film, that of the dutiful but "gentle" master.

The majority of the witnesses helped bolster this impression. A few would execrate him as a "coward" and a "gentleman bandit." But most, by comparing him to the bestial SS-men they had brushed against in the extermination camps, spoke of the Westerbork Commandant in temperate tones. Nevertheless, the trial was dull. Westerbork already was history. The camp stood empty. The "correct" Commandant, the "gentle" ruler of trains, received ten years imprisonment, with credit for the three and a half years he had already served.

2

Kurt

ADMINISTRATION

*Scene shifts to the office of the camp
Commandant. Conference at round table on
which statistical material on current production
figures . . . Tour of the "old" camp. Family
barracks. Camp Operations (Central Kitchen,
boiler room, bath house, hospital, etc.). The
camp Commandant moves with visitors or other
escorts through the various work-sites.
Inspection pause in the Statistical Office.*

From the film script of *Westerbork*

In the summer of 1943 Westerbork had a visitor who went about as Herr Wohl. A former Austrian officer, he had been put to work by an agency which had been sufficiently impressed with Westerbork to rank it as a "model camp." Herr Wohl was to study Westerbork and report on what made it, in the view of the agency, exceptional. From the Dutch example lessons might be drawn to make German camps elsewhere equally well-ordered and as faultless in filling transport quotas.

Wohl's report was an acutely "scientific" paper. Though grounded in the current racial assumptions, its objectivity could not be impugned. The investigator attributed Westerbork's efficiency to the high calibre of a small group of administrators; all German Jews, he pointed out. He stated that not even Gemmeker's office, the Camp High Command, could justly call itself the "executive organ of the daily administration," but that this function should be credited to the German-Jewish leadership. He singled out for special commendation the Chief Administrator, whom he identified as "No. 1."

"No. 1 is someone who has little about him of the typical Jew," he reported, "but all the more of the Prussian; someone with an extraordinary talent for organization, though accompanied by a total lack of scruples whenever his own interests or those of the Long-Term Residents are involved."

In his *dagboek*, Philip Mechanicus makes frequent mention of Kurt Schlesinger—Herr Wohl's "No. 1"—as the name synonymous with the business of the camp. It was the responsibility of Westerbork's Chief Administrator to deliver the required quotas for the trains to the East, and as such he had final authority in the making of the transport list. Gemmeker, on the night before the train's departure, would look over the list merely to ensure that it met the required number. "(Schlesinger) is an upstart," Mechanicus writes, "who has the power to do what he likes with the Jews."

It was as ruler of the "depressing transport business" that Schlesinger projected the aura of omnipotence noted by the diarist. A huge frame lent stature to the image. He had hands like millstones and a neck like a bull. His bald head was massive. Though barely forty, his face was fleshy, distinguished by a reddish "Hitler mustache," pale blue "phosphorescent" eyes, and sensually bloated lips.

In Westerbork Schlesinger was known as the "Jewish SS man" who struck terror in everyone. He usually wore a black army shirt, coarse brown riding breeches, blacktop boots and a Nazi-style cap. In cold weather he wore a long leather greatcoat. With the riding crop he sometimes carried he represented to the camp the fanatical German militarist—"arrogant," "self-assured," "uncouth," "cold." The inmates rumored that he had been a member of the *Schwarze Reichswehr*, the illegal paramilitary organization formed by German right-wingers after World War I.

But this identification with the enemy, though complete in all points of language, behavior, and dress, was spoiled by the badge which every inmate, even the Chief Administrator, must wear visibly on the chest. And inevitably, Schlesinger's cruel nemesis, the yellow star, thrust him back among the race he himself seemed to despise.

In the nineteenth century the province in which Westerbork was located had still been sufficiently remote, even in as small a country as Holland, that it could serve as a place of exile. In the isolation of Drente, Holland possessed its Siberia, where for a period petty criminals and paupers were sent to reclaim dismal "fen colonies" for agricultural use. Much of the fen and moor has since been seeded with grass, and rye and potato crops, orchards, pig raising and dairy farms have occupied the recovered grounds. Drente's capital, Assen, increased from a dreary village to a small marketing town with a flat, provincial look. Assen was about a half hour drive from Westerbork.

Within this desolation Westerbork's site could not have been less promising. At its groundbreaking in 1939 the farther neighborhood showed dun tracts of earth, churned and disked for the sprouting of the tuber. Adjacent to the camp the furze ran unspoiled, spilling over low sandy soil, twisting into mats of thorny growth overhung with agitated insect clouds. At the time of the camp's settlement, it was still possible to observe a remnant of the "reclaiming" race revealed in the distant silhouette of the peatcutter with his spade. And again, but beyond the camp's horizon, a sightseer might show himself clambering among the *hunnebedden*, the strange hoary boulder formations which were in reality funerary megaliths, marking Drente's famous "huns' graves," known to every Dutch child from his first school book. Apart from these rare human specks, the heath was empty.

But an altogether different atmosphere greeted Kurt Schlesinger, the man who would be Westerbork's Chief Administrator, when a year later he arrived on the same site. At this time, February, 1940, Westerbork was still known as the Central Camp for Refugees. It showed in those still tranquil days just three months before the invasion of Holland more than the rudiments of habitation and the beginnings of a "settled" look. The 750 German-Jewish refugees who lived there called it home. And proof of their adaptation was the distinct character that made itself noticeable in a pervasive, sour kitchen odor, in the sparkling windows of the barracks, and in the neat appearance of the tiny cottages. The main thoroughfare which at the height of the transports would be crowded with people was as yet innocent of its association with Boulevard des Misères. It looked raw, immense, with a few people walking or pedalling bicycles against the wind that blew off the moor. An occasional dray could be seen, and once in a while an automobile plunged and hobbled over the miserable ruts.

Prewar Westerbork was very much a German hamlet on Dutch soil, and Schlesinger here joined people whose experiences and circumstances paralleled his own. They were for the most part middle class professionals, merchants, small businessmen, and manufacturers; the men and women who later on, as Long-Term Residents, were to form the German-Jewish camp "aristocracy." As a group their solidarity was rooted in the humiliations they had shared. Their "settled" look was only apparent, and far from being reconciled to life in the refugee camp, they were consumed by bitterness and anger.

Schlesinger and his wife—a large, docile woman—had been held in different Dutch detention centers before being brought to Westerbork. Arrested at the Dutch-German border in January, 1939, they had been first interned in a bleak coastal depot where they were given a guilder a day, insufficient to buy the poor quality food, Schlesinger would later maintain with indignation. Almost all of Westerbork's "pioneers" had had similar experiences. From Holland they had hoped to go on to "further destinations," but no country in the world had wanted them, at least not in their plucked condition. Holland had refused them permanent entry, banishing them to oblivion in the heath. In Holland the same political and economic considerations prevailed as elsewhere, the same attitudes ranging from indifference to open hostility. Every refugee had his samples of insolent treatment at the hands of Dutch officials, stories of callousness and disrespect, of harassment and insults. They remembered the taunts—"Why, then, don't you go back to Germany?" or, "Would you rather be in a concentration camp?"

Westerbork's first residents felt forsaken by the world, cast out even by their own coreligionists. They were critical of the Jewish Refugee Committee established in 1933 to help the victims of Nazi persecution, and they accused the Dutch Jews of selfishness and blindness to their plight. In many of these the refugees sensed a silent reproach for their explusion, and in fact not a few Dutch Jews were of the opinion that they had probably deserved it.

Humiliation and revenge, history's endless cycle, were to be repeated in Westerbork between the group of embittered refugees and the Dutch Jews. Westerbork's other tragedy was the war of Jew against Jew which broke out when the refugee camp became a *Durchgangslager* practically run by the erstwhile outcasts. In a deposition during a postwar investigation Kurt Schlesinger testified to the feelings that motivated the camp's German-Jewish administrators in dealing with their Dutch brethren. "Because they had it better then," he stated, meaning the Dutch Jews before the war, "our belief was they must have it worse now."

Upon his arrival at Westerbork Kurt Schlesinger began humbly enough. Daily he went out with a shovel to dig ditches. But a small injury soon cut short his job with the ditchdigging detail. A vacancy existed in the office of the Westerbork branch of the Jewish Refugee Committee, and with the same fierce grip that had sustained the shovel, Schlesinger assumed the pen.

Meanwhile, external circumstances were changing the nature of Westerbork itself in a way that would have a crucial bearing on his own career. The camp's relative tranquility ended with the German conquest of Holland in the early weeks of May, 1940. Following a brief evacuation of the approximately seven hundred and fifty internees to northern Holland, and their return a few weeks later, the new wartime conditions at once made their effect felt in a reorganization of the camp.

In July the Central Camp for Refugees, as it was still known, was transferred from the Dutch Ministry of Justice. A Dutch Commandant was installed for the first time. His name was Captain Schol. By introducing measures which he considered beneficent and necessary, Captain Schol became the hapless contriver of Westerbork's bureaucratic machine which the Nazi command took over wholesale two years later, and which continued to function with abominable thoroughness until the very end of the war.

Previously Captain Schol had been posted in one of the distant Dutch colonies. The Dutch Jews intimate with him believed that he suffered from *tropenkolder*, a type of temporary madness native to the torrid zone. When the "fever" struck, Schol momentarily went berserk. At such times in Westerbork he was known to lash out at the inmates and harangue them fiercely. Though postwar testimony praised him for being uncompromisingly anti-Nazi, he was also rebuked for being a "poor judge of character." Some said that Westerbork was too much for him.

Schlesinger, on the other hand, was not at all insensitive to Schol's failings. As his work for the Jewish Refugee Committee dealt mostly with emigration matters, he maintained close and frequent contact with the Dutch soldier.

The stocky "pioneer" had a forceful personality and exerted every ounce of it on the simple captain. Schlesinger possessed in full what was known in camp parlance as *M.S.W.—Macht sich wichtig*—that is, "act the big shot." Though he had many rivals, no one among the inmates surpassed him in this art. Captain Schol, while conversing with the amiable clerk, had not the least idea that simultaneously a cloud of *M.S.W.* was impregnating the air. The soldier was clearly overmatched.

The effect of Schlesinger's persistent assaults on the tropical soldier became apparent in the first months of 1942. In the preceding year and a half the Dutch Commandant had demonstrated a penchant for military discipline. He had introduced a daily roll call. The able-bodied were divided into groups, each with a specific function. He had been insistent on a prompt, soldier-like bearing and had even set aside a *Strafbarak,* a punishment block, for violators of this code.

To all these measures Kurt Schlesinger lent a hearty acclaim. But as more and more Nazi officials turned up in Westerbork, and the camp's transfer into German hands became obviously imminent, Schlesinger made a worthy suggestion. He proposed to Schol that the Jewish inmates be allowed to participate in running the camp.

The reasons he advanced were eminently plausible. Schlesinger demonstrated the consequences to his—Schol's—own position if the Germans brought in their SS to administer the camp. He would be superseded. He would be an accomplice to the abandonment of Dutch authority. Would it not be better to forestall the Germans by anticipating all their demands? Only by presenting them with an operation so perfect in every detail that they would be foolish to object; by establishing a cohesively functioning organization, Schlesinger summed up, could the Nazis be deterred from imposing their rule on Westerbork.

The measures he propounded were also calculated to please the martial Dutchman. Schlesinger urged the laying down of firm controls. The inmates required total supervision. The camp fiber needed to be toughened. As for the latter, he reminded Schol of a barren plot within the perimeter, by far the coldest and windiest place in Westerbork. There, rather than indoors, as had been the current practice, the inmates must line up daily for roll calls. He also suggested the formation of a fire brigade and a Jewish police force, a uniformed squad patterned along military lines.

On March 1, 1942, Westerbork woke up to a series of orders from Commandant Schol. Two Jewish assistants—a coleader and deputy coleader—were assigned to each Dutch official in charge of an administrative department. Roll calls would no longer be held inside the Big Barrack, but outdoors, and had been advanced to the very early dawn. He further announced the establishment of a fire brigade. A camp police, the *Ordedienst* (Security Police), composed of twenty Jewish men, was also to commence its duties.

Kurt Schlesinger, given the title of Camp Elder, was made overseer of the newly appointed administrators.

On July 1, 1942, a few months after Schol's reorganization, Westerbork's populace watched the official entry of the German command. Nazi insignia sprouted in their midst. The SS guards had been brought in to augment the Dutch police contingent. They manned the watchtowers and guarded the gate. A fresh chapter in the camp's life had begun. The New Order had arrived. To what end no one knew.

One look at the German Commandant sufficed to unsettle the most optimistic. *Obersturmführer* Deppner looked like a murderer.

Two weeks after Deppner's arrival the transports commenced. July 15 and 16 were days of confusion and tumult such as Westerbork had not seen before. On both days a total of four hundred inmates—almost all German Jews—was ordered to join a transport of Jews from Amsterdam for the journey East. But it was not until after the trains had departed with their bewildered throng jammed into freight cars that a furor broke out among the *Alte Kampinsassen*. They felt betrayed by the Jewish Council.

The four hundred internees whom the train had taken on from Westerbork brought into the open suspicions harbored by the German Jews against the Jewish Council. In fact, the policy of this body was no secret. Its members had openly avowed their intent to place foreign Jews at the head of the lists demanded by the Central Office for Jewish Emigration, the Nazi branch dealing with "resettlement." Now, with their suspicions confirmed, the Long-Term Residents determined to prevail against the Jewish Council, against the Dutch Jews, against their very fate itself.

The ideal man to achieve their objective was Kurt Schlesinger. As *Dienstleiter* of the Jewish administrators he had ready access to the German Commandant, all the more so since the *Obersturmführer* demonstrated little interest in administration. Evidently, he considered it dull stuff compared to the entertainment he could have cursing and taunting his powerless victims. But the imprecations he was often heard to utter at the sight of a Jew were modified vis-à-vis Schlesinger.

In matters concerning the administration the German Commandant avoided Schol. Like all of Westerbork's Nazi officials he preferred to communicate through those who, as the disgruntled Dutch Jews put it, "understood their manner a little better." Schlesinger and Deppner understood each other. When the next transport left Westerbork, not one of the "pioneers" was on it. Nor would there be any on subsequent ones until the waning days of the transports.

This extraordinary feat had been accomplished by the simple expedient of "promoting" two thousand of the approximately three thousand German Jews who had been in the camp prior to July 1, 1942, to Long-Term Residents, that is, not liable to deportation. And with the elevation of the Long-Term Residents began the decline and eventual elimination of all Dutch influence in camp affairs. The eclipse of Captain Schol and his body of overseers came by degrees. Gradually the Dutch administrators were replaced by German-Jewish inmates. For a while Schol continued to function as the German Commandant's mouthpiece, merely setting his name to orders from above, until even the *Ordedienst*, his pride and joy, fell from his grasp. Sometime during Gemmeker's commandature the "poor judge of character" vanished from the camp.

The fall of the Jewish Council in Westerbork was swifter. Its collapse probably brought greater pleasure to the German Jews than their own triumphant elevation. In Amsterdam the Jewish Council would continue to perform messenger service for the German bureau in charge of Jewish "emigration," collecting lists of eligibles for Westerbork. But in Westerbork there was now a one-man Jewish Council who spoke German. In the aftermath of his successful palace coup Kurt Schlesinger had been installed as head of Administrative Section Two, the most important of Westerbork's departments.

Schlesinger's ascent proved him to be the "judge of character" Schol was not. He knew the Dutch Captain. He knew his Germans. He knew the toadies of the Jewish Council. He knew human nature, its weaknesses and failings, its venalities and fears. But one thing he knew best. He knew exactly what he wanted. He wanted to live, and toward that end his thirst for power was unqualified by either scruples or bounds.

As chief of *Dienstbereich* 2 he was in a position to wield power like an absolute monarch. For DB 2 stood at the nerve center of the camp. DB 2 *was* Westerbork, its *raison d'être*. Known in German as the *Verwaltung,* Schlesinger's department performed, in the words of its own 1943 year-end report, "all the general administrative functions, especially those related to the incoming and outgoing transports and all of the subsidiary tasks related to them."

Schlesinger had anticipated correctly. Not only was the SS kept out of Westerbork, as he had predicted to Schol, but Deppner granted the Long-Term Residents ever greater autonomy. During July, the first month of the transports, they handled seven trains ferrying 6,600 people. The trains came from Amsterdam, stopping briefly at the nearby station of Hooghalen (the spur connecting Westerbork to the main line was not laid until that winter) so that their wretched humanity might be registered; then they sped onward. The whole operation was brought off with a readiness that left no room to doubt the reliability and skills of the camp's original "settlers." From then on they were never in any danger of being replaced. They worked, they organized, they administered. When no other Jews were left, they organized and administered themselves out of existence.

DB 2, Schlesinger's department, was the nucleus of the twelve administrative units, including the *Lagerkommandatur,* the Camp High Command, by which Westerbork was governed. Under Schlesinger it reached a peak of perfection whereby the whole deportation process was reduced to no more than a collection of three-by-five index cards. At the height of the transports during 1943, Administrative Section Two contained twelve divisions. Of these, Division One, the General Administrative Services; Division Two, the Applications Office; and Division Eleven, the Central Card Catalogue, were directly involved in the preparation of transports.

The leaders of these three divisions labored mightily. Under the stimulus of *M.S.W.*, each tried to demean the others' function in the transport apparatus in order to glorify his own. Rudolf Fried, Schlesinger's deputy in DB 2, took credit for registering 53,703 Jews in the course of 1943. This was done under the General Administrative Services, which issued to each arrival distribution cards for food, clothing, and cigarettes as well as a camp pass. In addition, the General Administrative Services Department prepared catalogues for the Housing Office. It also supplied periodic listings of the inmate population to the German authorities outside the camp, primarily to the Security Police in the Hague and to the Central Office for Jewish Emigration in Amsterdam.

But the most important function of the General Administrative Services was to supply the *Zentralkartei*, the Central Card Index. Rudolf Fried proudly described the Central Card Index as the "focal point of all the administrative activities in the camp." He tinkered with this paper contrivance until he could demonstrate its absolute perfection. In the 1943 annual report the Central Card Index was said to have been so far improved and expanded that its card catalogue contained ten separate parts, each with its own catalogue leader.

The Central Card Index collected and processed the raw data furnished it by Division One, the General Administrative Services. On the basis of its own compilation the bureau then put together the weekly deportation lists. Fried spared no effort to keep the card catalogue up to date. He monitored the movements of the inmates from the moment of their arrival to the moment of their departure, encoding their statistics on individual cards, including grounds for exemption and actual exemptions. Division Twelve, the Statistical Office, prepared a daily numerical status report of the inmate population, so that at any time the Commandant might be told how many Jews were available for "resettlement to the East." It was not long, however, before the largest catalogue in the *Zentralkartei* was that marked "Departed." The cards in this file bore the deportee's final statistic: a stamp with the date of his departure.

The *Zentralkartei,* relying heavily on their information, had its tentacles deeply embedded in Westerbork's other administrative departments. Together the twelve departments operated what might have been a sizable municipality. In the space of roughly two years the Jewish officialdom registered more than one hundred thousand Jews. They housed, fed, and entertained them. They ministered to their health. They ran schools, nurseries, and an orphanage. The scores of workshops they operated ran the gamut from toy manufacturing to the stripping of downed airplanes. Buyers were dispatched throughout Holland to procure the necessities of camp life. Fuel was provided for the crematorium and hot water for the bathhouse, laundry, and kitchen. The bureaucrats made sure that order was kept, the garbage collected, the mail delivered, the warehouse supplied, and the canteen stocked. Their responsibilities ranged from operating the telephone system to general repair and maintenance, such as the upkeep of the barbed wire fence and the railroad tracks. But above all, they saw to it that the trains pulled out of Westerbork with the required number of "passengers," plus baggage and provisions for the long journey ahead.

These prodigious administrative feats were performed in an area no larger than a couple of oversized football fields. Since labor was free and, for a while at least, readily available, no hands were lacking to tend the trainloads of people that during the latter part of 1942 and all of the following year brought a constant influx to Westerbork. The Jews touched down briefly in the camp, usually one week but sometimes several. Some even remained a few months or, in rare cases, longer, though a great part barely stayed long enough to have their names put on the books.

To handle the 53,703 Jews who passed through Westerbork in 1943 the camp possessed a work force of approximately six thousand men and women, including a small group of Aryan employees. Of the Administrative Departments, the Metal Sector in that year employed the highest number (1,196), followed by the Health Service (1,128), the External Service (921), the

Work Shops (716), and the Women's Service (578). The Internal Service numbered 352 workers; the Technical Service, 286; Schools and Welfare, 284; the Security Police, 124. There were 59 workers in the Central Kitchen. Schlesinger's Department, DB 2, employed 382 people and the Camp High Command, 63.

In consequence of the ever present need to fill the trains, the numerical composition of the administrative departments, with the exception of the top leadership, fluctuated rather sharply. The numbers tended to remain fairly static, however, when Jews came pouring into Westerbork in a constant stream, as they did in 1943. But even in that year, despite the copious flow of "labor for the East," the roughly six thousand "permanent" camp residents represented a huge slice of Westerbork's population, considering that in the month of June the camp attained its highest occupancy rate of the entire war—13,541 people, crammed into barracks, designed to hold no more than half that number. This large pool of "permanents" represented the Commandant's "insurance," a human reservoir from which deportees might be drawn in order to fill out any transport that happened to fall short of its allotted number.

Westerbork's administrative structure, established by Schol and expanded by Deppner, was maintained in every important detail by the camp's last Commandant, Konrad Gemmeker. A trained administrator, unlike his predecessors, he readily saw the futility of tampering with something that functioned so extraordinarily well. By the time he arrived in early October, twenty-five transports totaling 23,000 Jews had departed from Westerbork under conditions that were, in the first few months of the "emigration," nothing less than chaotic. Only the dedicated zeal shown by the camp's Jewish leadership had managed to bring off the operation at all.

Under Gemmeker, in fact, Jewish rule in Westerbork became all-embracing. Though the Commandant himself presided over the *Lagerkommandatur*, its day-to-day operation was the work of his Jewish secretary, Herr Todtmann. Moreover, in August, 1943, the directorship of the camp passed in all but name into the hands of the Jewish leader who during Gemmeker's commandature had risen to the zenith of the camp establishment. At the peak of the transports, when weekly the train made its inroad, Gemmeker promoted Kurt Schlesinger to Chief Administrator, giving him absolute control over the entire administrative apparatus.

Schlesinger remained Chief Administrator until Westerbork's final day under Nazi rule. On April 12, 1945, Konrad Gemmeker, by means of a symbolic accolade, the rendering of his 6.35 mm pistol, officially placed the camp under Kurt Schlesinger's command.

Schlesinger was far from being Westerbork's only example of Nazi-Jewish osmosis, though he showed the fruition at its crudest. The type happened to be rife among the administrative bigwigs, epigones in dress, manner, and speech of those who plotted their destruction. Having become inured to camp life over the years of their captivity, sharing moreover with Westerbork's Nazis an antipathy towards the Dutch and Dutch Jews, they identified with the oppressor to a degree that was both comic and revolting. The majority of the camp elite would probably have seen nothing odd in the words with which Schlesinger chastised a Jewish official of Westerbork's Welfare Department who expressed some cautious reservations about the *Ordedienst*.

"You look at everything through Jewish glasses," the Chief Administrator told him. He accused the man of being "too idealistic." "I," Schlesinger said, "as leader of the camp, see things in a different light and, above all, have to make sure that there is order." But, in fact, the point this official, Joseph Weisz, had made—that the camp police some day might well be used to help the Nazis round up Jews—was clear-sighted enough, despite the "Jewish glasses."

Section Three, the Camp Security Police, had only too well answered the object of its creator, Captain Schol. No German SS had entered Westerbork; instead there had come a "Jewish SS," the *Ordedienst*. Arthur Pisk, chief of the OD, among his fellow Jews had the distinction of being the "most hated man in the camp."

A former Austrian officer, Pisk had been appointed by Captain Schol. Pisk, too, affected the Hitler mustache, the breeches, boots, the crop, and assorted leather. With his coal-black hair and eyes, Mechanicus thought he resembled a pirate.

Under Pisk the small squad of twenty men, eighteen German and two Dutch Jews, had expanded a year after its founding into a force of almost two hundred, about equally divided between Dutch and German-speaking Jews. The unit which Schol had been proud to trot out for review was transformed into a vicious military tool. Schol had dressed its members in brown overalls with a red armband. For Pisk the unit fell in wearing jackboots and a green uniform similar to that of the Nazi Green Police, Holland's most notorious Jew hunters. The Jewish star was sown onto the left breastpocket of the uniform, immediately below the OD insignia.

Captain Schol had established the OD for the purpose of maintaining quiet and order in the camp. But as the transports began to roll, the OD was given duties not unlike those performed by the regular SS in other camps. Westerbork's Jewish policemen patrolled the camp gate. They guarded the punishment barracks and surveilled the labor details working outside the camp. They kept an eye on the canteen and warehouse. They helped man the fire-fighting squad, an air defense unit, and the stretcher-bearing brigade. And what Weisz had feared came to pass: they assisted with the deportations.

On "transport" days the OD laid its normal duties aside to load the waiting train with human beings. Their day began at dawn with small detachments collecting the children from the orphanage. The stretcher-bearing brigade fetched the sick from the hospital. Others, at approximately seven o'clock, escorted the healthy inmates to the train and commenced the loading. About four hours later, the train having been filled, the OD's work was done. On days of unusually large transports, the OD could call on the Emergency Squad, the *Notbereitschaft*, created specifically for that purpose. And if the combined strength of the OD and the Emergency Squad, which in 1943 consisted of about one hundred men, still proved insufficient, the OD could activate the camp's baggage detail, the Flying Column.

In recompense for the readiness with which it toiled—OD members worked round the clock on ten-hour shifts six days a week; it "never slept," was the motto—Pisk's regiment was honored with the fullest confidence of the Commandant. So complete was his trust that Gemmeker did not hesitate to employ his Jewish soldiers in "actions" away from the camp. One January day in 1943, one hundred of them were sent to Apeldoorn, a town in central Holland, to assist the regular German police with the "evacuation" of a Jewish mental institution. From all accounts, they vied in brutality with the Nazis. Pisk's men swept through the wards, jerking patients from their beds amidst a pandemonium of screams. Without allowing many of them to dress, the OD men shoved the terrified inmates out into the icy night. Vans were waiting to rush them to the train, by which they were taken directly to Auschwitz. Six months later Gemmeker dispatched another detachment of 120 men from Westerbork to Amsterdam, where during the evening of June 20 they helped the Green Police round up 5,600 of their fellow Jews.

As daily they witnessed the outrages committed by the OD, the captives of Westerbork feared and detested its members with a passionate intensity. Because it was revolting to see fellow Jews doing the work of the common enemy and because in Westerbork they did not meet with a like brutality from the Germans, the inmates ironically came to regard the OD as a greater ill than the SS itself. Like the SS the camp's Security Police were a ragtag rabble of misfits, *Lumpen*, and pathological cases. A good portion of the OD men, wrote Mechanicus, had been "recruited from the dregs of Jewish society, rough, coarse fellows, without refinement, human feelings or compassion; they just live for their cigarettes and for an easy affair with women like themselves."

But at no time was the spectacle of Jew spoiling Jew more glaringly repellent than on "transport" days when Pisk's uniformed minions put the deportees on the train. Whatever final hopes of reprieve or miracle the mass huddled on the platform might have had were quickly scotched by the merciless zeal of the OD men. Not only were they impatient of the least delay, impervious to the most innocent appeal, but they also allowed nothing to escape their vigilance. The head of the camp's orphanage, H. Birnbaum, recalled after the war how the OD thwarted his attempt to snatch a four-year-old from a departing transport. As Birnbaum proceeded to pry the boy from the train, an OD man hurried over and foiled him. Summoned to the OD office, Birnbaum was severely reprimanded. Not long after this incident, when all the children of the orphanage were shipped to Auschwitz, Birnbaum volunteered to accompany them rather than stay behind in Westerbork.

If Gemmeker was the most treacherous man in Westerbork, Schlesinger the most feared, and Pisk the most hated, the sobriquet "most mysterious" might be fitted to Dr. F. M. Spanier, the director of Westerbork's most anomalous institution. He ran a hospital that at the height of its operation was the largest to be found in wartime Holland.

Dr. Spanier and his wife had obtained a sort of anonymous fame, the type embracing not individuals but the disaster of which they are a helpless part. In the late spring of 1939 the name *St. Louis* became a familiar symbol of the "displaced person" to whom the earth is barred because he has no papers. The *St. Louis* was the ship which roamed the seas in a vain search for a country prepared to accept the 937 German-Jewish refugees it had on board. Rebuffed at every port in the Americas, including the United States, the refugees steamed back to Europe, where at last, yielding to public sentiment, several governments agreed to admit the stateless wanderers. One of those countries was Holland, and among the 181 passengers to whom it granted asylum were Dr. Spanier and his wfie. Both arrived in Westerbork not long afterwards.

Some four years later Dr. Spanier operated a medical complex that in size alone would do justice to any modern metropolis. By the end of 1943 the camp hospital with its 1,800 beds, 120 doctors and a staff of more than 1,000—completely Jewish—was among the largest in all of occupied Europe. No doubt the existence of this fine hospital served to allay Jewish apprehensions concerning their future in the East. Why, after all, should the Nazis take such good care of them if they intended to kill them further down the road?

The medical team comprised a phalanx of skill second to none. Through the narrow passages of the hospital barracks circulated orthopedists and surgeons, specialists for every vital organ, neurologists, dentists, psychiatrists and psychologists, supported by a staff of nurses, masseurs, dieticians, dental assistants, X-ray and lab technicians. The hospital work shop made medical instruments, shoe supports, trusses, and artificial limbs. The hospital's drug cabinets bulged with pills and potions from the State Magazine for Drugs. The outpatient clinic, pharmacy, and quarantine station were open to the public twenty-four hours a day, as were the First Aid Stations the hospital operated outside the medical complex.

Because of its extensiveness, but more so because of the power its director wielded, Westerbork's medical empire has been called a "state within a state." For in the hospital compound, Spanier's authority was absolute, overshadowing even the Commandant's. Indeed, the extraordinary hold Dr. Spanier seemed to have over the camp's top Nazi official was seen as the key to his omnipotence. Ordinarily, Gemmeker had but to reach for his coat and the camp's most powerful Jewish officials would instantly play the valet. But when the Commandant entered Spanier's office, the doctor did not deign to rise from his chair.

Where did Dr. Spanier get this power? Both men hailed from Düsseldorf and much was made of that among the inmates. All sorts of other suppositions were advanced, but none helped shed any light on the unaccountable connection between the two men. Only one thing was certain: when Dr. Spanier gave an exemption, no one could take it away.

Dr. Spanier stood at the top of the index by which Westerbork measured a person's worth: his power to wrest a living soul from the transport. Unlike the reprieves granted by Schlesinger, always provisional at best, when Dr. Spanier put his signature to an exemption not even the Commandant would dare override it. By the same token, the withdrawal of his protection was attended by the same unalterable finality. "From now on I will no longer protect you"—these words were an absolute decree from which there was no appeal. The person who crossed him was doomed. Elie Cohen, a member of his staff, was so doomed because his wife had uttered a mild insult to a German Jew. "From now on I will no longer protect you," prepared their way to Auschwitz. "No one questions his medical ability," wrote Herr Wohl about Dr. Spanier—identified as "No. 8" in his report—"but there is some question as to his humanity."

Herr Wohl's characterization of Dr. Spanier was among the more flattering of the profiles he limned of Westerbork's upper crust. Apart from the few he typified as being "correct" or "least to be influenced," his relentless digging and probling uncovered a veritable rogue's gallery of tyrants, upstarts, connivers, skirt chasers, sadists, bullies, and power maniacs. Small wonder Herr Wohl isolated "corruption" as the pervasive element in Westerbork's life at the top. No moral criticism was implied in this finding, as befitted a "scientific" study. Evidently, Wohl regarded the venality he found to be rife among Schlesinger and his cohorts a Semitic trait it would be pointless to stigmatize. In fact, Herr Wohl might have gone further and added that if corruption seemed to thrive more vigorously at the top, it was only because of greater opportunities and higher visibility. For in Westerbork the morality of almost everyone sooner or later perished. Westerbork was a community of pariahs, an amorphous band of alienated, desperate individuals with their ears cocked to the sound of the trains. In everyone's battle for survival the notions of civilized existence were stamped into the ground. Good and evil here were narrowed down to the single criterion of having one's name on or off the weekly deportation list. As in the primal state of nature, every Jew sought to save his own skin with any means at his disposal, and it is highly improbable that the course of those outside the camp establishment—mainly the Dutch Jews—had they been suddenly elevated to the elite, would have differed from the leaders they execrated.

Had he looked beyond the "corruption" of the administrative hierarchs, Herr Wohl might have noted that Westerbork as a whole was a morass of egotism, greed and rancor, in which the lower ranks were obsessed with malevolence toward the higher. To the unprivileged, Westerbork's Jewish chieftains formed an exclusive club which stood as a permanent incitement to their envy. The camp's elite lived segregated from the rest of the inmates in small cottages. They had the liberty to prepare their own food, while their less fortunate brethren ate what was given them from the Central Kitchen. At the same time, because they exercised power over life and death, they were fawned over like royalty. Once, when Schlesinger broke his leg in a bicycle collision with, of all people, the Commandant, half the camp—even Gemmeker himself—rushed to his hospital bed. His well-wishers, laden with gifts and snacks, actually fought for the honor of inscribing his cast, even though the "Jewish SS man" was universally detested.

In psychoanalysis, "abreaction" takes place when a person relieves his repressed emotions. Herr Wohl, having trained his scientific eye on Westerbork's leading specimens of Jewish corruption, believed the moral obloquy he found in them to be due to the "abreacting of inferiority complexes." Wohl viewed their inferiority complexes as stemming from prolonged internment and degradation. However, the Austrian would have had to go back no farther than 1933, the year Hitler came to power in Germany, to come up with a simpler explanation for the psychological phenomena that attend human degradation. For years on end it had been dinned into German Jews that they were *Untermenschen*, those subsisting outside the pale of humanity. They had been robbed of their goods and stripped of their individual identity. Later, in their Dutch exile, a large number of them had become dependent on others for their sustenance, living on handouts or forced to take jobs they considered to be beneath their dignity. At last, adding insult to injury, they had been shipped to Westerbork, many of them even before a single German soldier had set foot on Dutch soil.

Yet the venality of the Jewish leaders, as Wohl no doubt understood, was part and parcel of the system by which the Germans allowed Westerbork to be governed. A Hobbesian war of all against all among the inmates, stimulated by the corrupt excesses of the Jewish elite, served to deflect hatred from the common oppressor and was the chief reason for the camp's "model status" which had sent Herr Wohl to Westerbork in the first place. And Herr Wohl had been very pleased with what he saw of the "executive" organ.

Had Westerbork's bureaucrats seen his report, though they

would have found his psychological profiles objectionable, they would doubtlessly have taken immense pride in Wohl's kudos. Long immersed in an element that had warped them, they survived on cards and catalogues. They had completely lost sight of their own end—self-preservation. They had been absorbed by a machine that had become indifferent to the object it was intended to serve.

Though the camp's Jewish leaders might argue that by their labors they had succeeded in keeping a large scale SS presence out of Westerbork, the only benefactors of their visionary reasoning were the Germans. Not only was the Nazi command spared a considerable expenditure in manpower, but by having Jews at the camp controls they managed to promote a sense of security among the inmates which contributed to the dispatch of the deportation process.

3

Philip

INMATE

Scene shifts to main road in the direction of the "new" camp. The large barracks, industrial activities. The camp in its current state is shown in all of its parts. Variety of jobs in work units: workshops, industrial sector, external service, farmstead. The life of the inmates: work, living conditions, leisure activities.

From the film script of *Westerbork*

Philip Mechanicus' index card at the *Registratur* stated that he was fifty-three years old; that he had entered Westerbork on November 7, 1942 as an *"S-Fall,"* a punishment case, via the concentration camp at Amersfoort; that there were no other family members; and, because of his delinquent status, no permissible grounds for exemption.

A death warrant could not have been more explicit. With these "credentials," the former journalist might as easily have put himself on the next train to Poland as await the list makers' tally. But instead of boarding a grimy freight car bursting with his fellow Jews, he soon found himself more or less comfortably lodged in the camp hospital. A month in the concentration camp of Amersfoort had put him there, and there he would remain in convalescence for the next nine months.

Mechanicus purposely drew out his stay as long as possible, deploying his illness as a kind of surrogate exemption. As his condition improved, he began taking stock of the world around him. Soon he was sufficiently recovered to be allowed, by special permission, to roam the camp at will, months before his actual release from the hospital. Back in his bed, propped up against the pillows, he put down what he had seen and heard.

In Westerbork Mechanicus felt himself plunged into an apocalyptic disaster. He saw a few people rise to moral eminence. He saw the majority sink to the primordial state. What he observed filled him equally with abhorrence and compassion. Westerbork both repelled and excited an inexhaustible curiosity which filled his *dagboek* to overflowing. "I feel," he wrote in his diary on Saturday, May 29, 1943,

> as if I am an official reporter giving an account of a shipwreck. We are all together in a cyclone and feel the holed ship slowly sinking. We try to reach a harbor, but that harbor seems far away. The idea is gradually forming in my mind that I have not been brought here by my *persecutors,* but that I have gone on the journey *voluntarily* in order to do my work. I am busy all day long and am never bored for a single minute; sometmes the days actually seem too short. Duty is duty and work is ennobling. I write during a great part of the

day. Sometimes I begin at half past five in the morning and sometimes I am still busy in the evening after bedtime, gathering my impressions and experiences for the day.

Spare, introspective, and modest, with his beret and pipe, Mechanicus looked the middle-aged European man of letters. He had been a newspaper reporter and editor before coming to Westerbork as an S-detainee, having been arrested in Amsterdam for not wearing the star. His series on Soviet Russia and Palestine, both later published in book form, were distinguished by a characteristic blend of objective, conscientious, and insightful reportage—journalism at its best. These qualities served him well in Westerbork. They enabled him, despite his personal involvement, to write a most perceptive eye witness account of what Westerbork was like and what it was like to be in Westerbork. The diary he kept was published in Holland by the title *In Depot*, and translated into English as *Year of Fear: A Jewish Prisoner Waits for Auschwitz*.

But in Westerbork Mechanicus was no longer a reporter with a deadline. He was just another inmate trying to keep from being deported—a next to impossible task for an *S-Fall*. But thanks to a mysterious benefactor, the *S* somehow disappeared in the course of his stay in the hospital. From then until his deportation in early 1944, Mechanicus thought and breathed *Sperre*—exemption—pledging body and soul to the unequal contest with the transport.

The day of dread was not long in coming. On July 4, 1943, a Sunday, Mechanicus learned that his name would be entered on the list for that Tuesday's transport. He straightaway headed for the office of Dr. Spanier, the person he suspected of having liquidated his *S*. But Dr. Spanier was nowhere to be found. The medical chief had a habit of making himself scarce whenever a transport was about to leave and hordes of desperate inmates stalked his every move. At the office of the Jewish Council Mechanicus suffered another rebuff. Next he attempted to obtain some papers demonstrating his eligibility for the Puttkammer emigration list, an exemption for Jews with access to foreign currency. At last, still at sea, he sought out "a little old gentleman with a pointed beard," Herr Trottel by name. An authentic M.S.W.'r, Herr Trottel boasted of his hold over Schlesinger and his good relations with the Commandant. Leave everything to me, he assured Mechanicus.

That same evening "the Great Man" himself swung by the hospital ward, looking for Mechanicus. Why had he "taken so long to put [his] affairs in order?" the Chief Administrator wanted to know. He must promise to do more for himself in the future.

The diarist did not quite know what to make of this brusque encounter, so he was not altogether surprised when next day his name appeared on the transport list just the same. He took the news calmly. Esther Hillesum, who came to say goodbye, remarked on his serenity. He was standing up straight, fully packed, and ready to go. Neither of them mentioned the train. Mechanicus read her some of the things he had written and they "philosophized a bit." They laughed, and said they would see each other again.

It was not until late Tuesday morning, mere hours before the train's departure, that Mechanicus was finally notified that his name had been deleted from the transport, a large one containing 2,600. "Congratulations from all sides—handshakes from my nearest neighbors. I received the expressions of sympathetic interest with a smile. Deep down I felt sorrow—everywhere around other men were being summoned out of their beds and told to prepare for the sinister transport. The congratulations must have been like a slap in the face for those who were going."

Next day, Mechanicus again met with Trottel, bringing him fifteen cigarettes. "He accepted them with the excuse that he himself had offered cigarettes on my behalf." Trottel advised him to have his place on the Puttkammer list confirmed. He also instructed Mechanicus, two days later, to go to Schlesinger and "make it clear to him that he will have some say in what you publish later about Westerbork."

No sooner had he returned from this rendezvous than he was wanted at the *Registratur*, where Fräulein Slottke was waiting for him. Fräulein Slottke, the IVB4 official in charge of monitoring exemption requests, came straight to the point: what was his marital status and what sort of writing had he done at the *Algemeen Handelsblad*? He was divorced, Mechanicus replied, but his wife had been Aryan and he had a half-Aryan daughter. As for his writing, he carefully answered that he had done "literary work in general."

On July 10, Mechanicus, accompanied by Trottel, was received by Schlesinger. After thanking him for his help and having hinted that he would do something in return at the appropriate time, he told his powerful patron about his interview with Fräulein Slottke. Schlesinger thought it looked promising because Slottke dealt with exemptees for Theresienstadt, and asked Mechanicus to return with "a few lines about your career and your contact abroad some time tomorrow." Five days later the diarist was notified that he had been granted a blue Z stamp (Z—*Zurückstellung*—deferment), certifying that he was exempted "until further notice" and entitling him, among other benefits, to a smoker's card and 250 guilders spending money.

A veteran of Westerbork, Mechanicus harbored no illusions about the reliability of his *Sperre*. In his own wry definition, an exemption list was nothing more than "a collection of Jews who will one day be deported." The aptness of this definition was quickly demonstrated in his own case for a mere four days after taking possession of his Z, Trottel informed him that he had been removed from the Theresienstadt list—but not to worry because Schlesinger was sure to look after him.

When less than two months later the Commandant, compiling the deportation list himself, put Mechanicus down for the transport of September 14, the Chief Administrator once more came to the rescue, though again at the eleventh hour. As Mechanicus stood beside the panting train, fully packed and about to embark, he was spotted by Dr. Ottenstein, the Jewish official at Westerbork in charge of examining exemption requests. Instructing him not to get on, Ottenstein raced off to fetch Schlesinger, with whom he returned almost at once. The Chief Administrator, ramming a letter into the diarist's hands, ordered him to the *Registratur* and told him to stay there until the train's departure.

It was this experience, the second close call in as many months, that impelled Mechanicus to redouble his exemption efforts. Within days he applied for a *Sperre* based on his dis-solved marriage and half-Aryan offspring. Two weeks later he collected his second blue Z stamp, again qualifying him for Theresienstadt.

Pragmatist that he was, he then filed for Aryanization.

> I took a look at myself with this in mind. My nose is not that curved, I have thin lips and my name can easily pass for that of an Aryan . . . There is no disgrace about passing oneself off as an Aryan, although it is not pleasant to accept a gift of the oppressor. The main thing is to get out of his clutches.

Finally he registered with Weinreb, the Jewish "emigration expert" whose exemption list was then all the rage.

But all of these activities bought him little more than a month's respite before his name again came up for a Theresien-stadt transport. This time, however, it was Dr. Ottenstein who took him off the hook. Everything was fine, the exemption officer told Mechanicus after calling the Hague about his Aryani-zation request; he did not have to go. Mechanicus later learned that his petition had never even been submitted, leading him to wonder whether Ottenstein had actually called the Hague or had merely pretended to have done so. "From this small inci-dent," observed the diarist, "one can see that there are many ways of saving a person from deportation."

But no one intervened on March 8, 1944, the day he was put on the train for Bergen-Belsen. In October he was moved to Auschwitz-Birkenau. There he was taken out and shot.

When first granted a blue Z stamp Mechanicus remarked, "I have been moved up a whole class." What he meant was that the *Sperre* had lifted him from those without exemptions at the bottom of the social heap to the "middle class" of blue Z holders whose departure had been stayed "until further notice."

In Westerbork, as everyone there soon learned, the preemi-nent class consisted of those inmates who could boast an ex-emption from the transports. All of the camp's luminaries, for example, had camp cards on which the letters *ST* stood out in bold red. These letters proclaimed that the bearer could not be peremptorily deported as his name had been entered on the Commandant's personal exemption list—the so-called Basic List (*Stamlijst* in Dutch).

The Basic List, the crown jewel of exemptions, had come into existence while Deppner, the whip-wielding alcoholic, was Commandant. On it doted two thousand German Jews—Westerbork's Long-Term Residents, whose internment predated the German takeover on July 1, 1942. Succeeding commandatures maintained this privileged caste, though in September of 1943 Gemmeker slashed the total, which now included some Dutch Jews as well, in half. Apart from a handful on that list who were never deported at all, the half that survived the Commandant's purge managed to stay on at Westerbork until the very last transports.

By creating this list Deppner followed a model that without exception formed the social structure in every German concentration camp: a small elite set against a powerless Jewish commonality. In the case of Westerbork, the German Jew was pitted against the Dutch Jew, the privileged against the unprivileged—in fact, those who were to live against those who were to die. The internal tensions flowing from this strife generated a state of electric tumult among the camp dwellers while leaving the Nazi rulers in a vacuum from which they could pursue their ends without perturbation.

Jews whose exemptions situated them in the "middle class" were far less successful than the *ST* stamp holders in hanging on to their *Sperres*. Covering a broad range, grounds for exemption in this intermediate social strataum ran the gamut from being married to a non-Jew to having opted for Protestantism before January 1, 1941, and from "contributing" to the Reich war chest to being able to claim foreign or dual nationality. Although most of the dual nationals were Dutch Jews who had never strayed beyond their own borders, their passports proclaimed them to be citizens of both Holland and some other country, usually in Central or South America. They had simply purchased their Latin American passports through intermediaries when that still proved possible. (Oddly enough, the Nazis for the longest time continued to recognize passports so acquired as valid, much as they appeared to take seriously the spurious claim to Portuguese citizenship of Holland's Sephardic community. But as neither condition held up for long, both groups were eventually bundled off to the East.)

Also belonging to the "middle class" were the Puttkammer candidates and the participants in the Calmeyer list. Calmeyer was the German lawyer who had the job of examining the blood credentials of Jews claiming to be Aryans. To qualify, the prospective Aryan was required to submit proof of Aryan ancestry on one side and could not be married to a Jew or have been a member of the Jewish religious community before May 10, 1940, the day of the German invasion. In this class, too, were gathered the bulk of the administration's petty bureaucrats, for which favor most of them could thank their friends higher up; the "Cultural Jews" collectively known as the *Barnevelders*; the "Palestine Jews" earmarked for exchange with German nationals in Allied hands; German Jews who had distinguished themselves in battle during World War I; workers employed in the so-called "vital industries" of shoemaking, clothing manufacturing, and metal sorting; and those Dutch and German Jews whose international business connections the Nazis might yet wish to exploit. All of the inmates thus consigned to the middle class were issued blue exemption stamps, except the "vital workers," who received green ones.

In time, as the once copious flow of "transport-free material"—"freed" for, not from transport—began drying up, the middle class emerged as numerically dominant in Westerbork. In the winter of 1943–44, it accounted for roughly two-thirds of the camp's 9,000 Jews, outnumbering the nonexempt—Westerbork's "proletariat"—by a ratio of three to one.

As in conventional class society, so in Westerbork class differences manifested themselves all along the social spectrum. The camp's Long-Term Residents not only lived, ate, and dressed better than the proletariat, they also anticipated a qualitatively superior resolution of their Westerbork internment. Not for them Auschwitz, the dumping-ground of the unexempted, but the reputed comforts of Theresienstadt, the "Model Camp" in the Bohemian forest. Eventually about 5,000 Jews from the Dutch transit camp—*ST* recipients, *Barnevelders*, "Protestants," and German nationals with documented proof of their sacrifices on behalf of their fatherland during the Great War—were to pass through the gate of this "baroque little fortress town," most of whom survived the war.

The class lines between Westerbork's aristocrats, the Basic List incumbents, and their social inferiors tended to remain fixed and respected, not infrequently up until the very moment of departure. For not only did it sometimes happen that Long-Term Residents left Westerbork in regular passenger trains, traveling third class, but what is more, left it with complimentary rations of cigarettes, butter, soap powder, sugar, and jam— "luxury" items never to be found aboard the cattle cars conveying just about everybody else.

Westerbork's peculiar pecking order yielded an equally peculiar strain of class consciousness. Originating in the instinct of self-preservation, class feelings exuded the miasma of a rapidly decomposing social order. Thus, perhaps to stifle their own fears, the exempt habitually fixed Poland as a uniquely proletarian destiny. By the same token, few things made Westerbork's plebeians happier than seeing their "betters" relegated to the proletrian fold. When in September of 1943 rumors began flying that the camp was closing down and all Jews were to be "evacuated" to the East, Mechanicus noted that the mood in the camp was actually joyful.

Such effusions of class awareness, however warped, might well attest to the presence of a strong quotient of class solidarity, were it not for the fact that this was Westerbork and *sauve qui peut*. Jews on the Basic List fought like dogs to keep their caste closed and privileges in tact. Its membership existed at the pleasure of the Commandant and did not change except at his behest. But the iron laws of the Final Solution played havoc with the lives of nearly all of the other exemptees, ultimately pressing virtually every one of them into the ranks of the proletariat. The lines between the lowest and intermediate echelons were utterly flexible and much depended on whether or not a new prisoner would be shipped out immediately upon, or shortly after, arrival. For at Westerbork, as in other camps, the longer one managed to hold out, the better were the chances of survival, which in this camp was synonymous with having one's deportation stayed *bis auf weiteres*—until further notice.

Westerbork's Jews left few stones unturned in their quest to keep the Angel of Death at bay. Much as in normal life people take out insurance against all potential hazards, so inmates tried to cover themselves on as many fronts as possible. But in Westerbork, where no one could ever be sure of the ground under his feet, such perspicacity rarely paid off and might actually backfire. That happened to someone Dr. Ottenstein knew. The inmate in question had a place on the Basic List, a South American passport, and a Palestine Certificate. He then tried to complete his coverage with a certificate of baptism. Having created a conflict with his Palestine exemption, the administration wasted no time in dispatching him eastward.

"[W]e Jews," wrote Mechanicus, "grasp at every straw in order to avoid the journey to Poland." But what Poland actually signified the Jews in Westerbork would not be told, for throughout the war they seemed to have remained quite unaware of what was happening there. And the less they knew, the more they speculated. As reported by Mechanicus, attitudes ranged from cautious optimism to flat despair.

Though nowhere a luxuriant growth, optimism was most firmly rooted in the young and able-bodied, in people used to working with their hands. Inclined more than others to believe in the reigning Nazi fiction that Jews were being shipped to Poland to work, they were also more confident of survival. Mechanicus especially detected this hopeful attitude among the young men and women of the *Hashera*, the Zionist youth organization which groomed Jews for a life of toil in Palestine. He thought that these young people, with their natural exuberance, stood a good chance of prevailing in Poland, provided they were given a "reasonable chance."

Far less sanguine about their chances in the East were Westerbork's women and older inmates, the women because they were worried about their children and babies; the older inmates because they were no longer young and strong. Intellectuals, too, feared the worst. Nothing in their past had prepared them to live by the sweat of their brow—if indeed they were being sent to "work-camps," which in view of the Nazi contempt for intellectuals, especially Jewish intellectuals, many of them doubted.

Equally pessimistic were those who had already spent time in Nazi concentration camps prior to coming to Westerbork, though one inmate, a former internee of Vught, stated that he'd rather be off to Poland than go back to Vught. Nothing, he said, could be worse.

But what filled every Jew with trepidation was the inhuman conditions under which they were being deported. Few, however, dared look beyond the funeral arrangements into the grave itself. The man found gazing at the trench that ringed the camp was an exception. He ventured that at the end of the war the Germans would have no qualms about perpetrating another Katyn in Westerbork. Most bystanders, Mechanicus among them, disagreed, contending that the slaughter of 4,500 Polish officers at Katyn had been the work of Bolsheviks. But later, alone with his diary, Mechanicus came to doubt his own words and no longer entirely excluded the possibility of German atrocities on the scale of Katyn.

However much opinion may have differed on Poland, it was only after the war that anyone would admit to having known about the gassing. One who said he knew was Dr. Elie Cohen. Dr. Cohen, a survivor of Auschwitz and the author of a study of human behavior in the concentration camp, claimed that people in Westerbork knew that Jews were being gassed in the East but repressed the thought. He himself had heard rumors "about the gassing of Polish Jews" when he was still in Westerbork, and the Jews there, he recalled, fully expected the same thing to happen to their own sick and aged. "That in spite of all this," affirmed Cohen in *Human Behavior in the Concentration Camp*, "the thought of gassing was repressed seems to me beyond any doubt."

It may well be, as Cohen asserts, that the Jews in Westerbork repressed the thought of gassing and that this repression or denial accounts for the terrible dread Poland evoked in the inmates. But the fact remains that no one at the time even

66

obliquely alluded to it, and as late as January, 1944, Mechanicus could unequivocally write, "People still do not know what happens to the deported Jews in Poland."

The Jews in camp Westerbork had nothing in common but a biological condition whose imprint, the six-pointed star, was worn chest-high on the outer garment like a second heart. " . . . [I]t is here not exactly," wrote Esther Hilllesum in December, 1942, "what one could call an organically grown community with a regular breathing. And yet—and that is what is so amazing—in it are duplicated all of the aspects, classes, isms, contradictions and currents of normal society . . . But what strikes one again and again is that despite the communal misery the contradictions remain alive."

The diversity among the inmates was indeed striking. For aside from the Dutch and German Jews, who accounted for the majority, Westerbork also boasted colonies of Czech, Polish, Rumanian, Hungarian, Russian, Turkish, Spanish, and Italian Jews. There were full Jews, Protestant Jews, Catholic Jews, and "White" Jews, that is, Gentiles whom the Nazis had caught aiding Jews and punished with internment. Westerbork had gypsies and bead-fingering nuns and priests, their yellow stars lending an incongruous sparkle to their somber habits. It had Jews representing every shade of religious opinion and observance, as well as those without any, the majority. It had children, adolescents, adults, and hoary men and women from rest homes. It had Jews with chronic ailments, invalids, and Jews from mental institutions and prisons. Westerbork even had a small number of Jewish Nazis—whom the Commandant personally ordered deported after it became known to him that they had complained about his leniency towards Jews.

The haphazard quilting of thousands of disparate individuals, each threatened with destruction, was no small contributor to that "war of nerves" Dr. Ottenstein identified as the quintessence of Westerbork. Nationality conflicts generated much of the friction. Most disruptive of all was the bitterness that marked the relationship between Dutch and German Jews.

Long-simmering, their conflict quickly came to a boil in Westerbork's overwrought emotional atmosphere. What rankled the Dutch Jews was not just that the camp's "pioneers" had swept to power on the coattails of a Commandant who evidently preferred dealing with those "whose manner (he) probably understood a little better"; nor that they wielded that power arbitrarily and ruthlessly, threatening or punishing with deportation anyone they bore a pique; nor even that they made a parade of the ornaments of power—better housing, food, and clothing, and, most important of all, apparent immunity from deportation. Rather, the Dutch Jews hated the German Jews because by their lights they were Germans first and Jews second, and, withal, depressingly similar to their Aryan oppressors.

The German Jews were also far more accessible targets for their throttled anger. When a Dutch Jew beheld a German Jew he did not see the victim he was himself. He saw a strutter, a mountebank, a demon for order, alternately bellowing or groveling, depending on whether he was in the saddle or under it. What he saw, in other words, was a stereotypical Teuton. The Dutch Jews said that the German Jews had all the faults of the Prussians and the Jews rolled in one.

Conversely, the sight of Dutch Jews triggered unpleasant memories in the German Jew. It served to remind him of how little had been done for him prior to the outbreak of war, and with what equanimity Dutch Jews had watched their government shuffle him off to Westerbork. But most of all, the German Jew thought of July, 1942, when the Jewish Council, on the theory that foreign Jews should be the first to go, placed approximately four hundred of his kind on the two initial transport trains that left Amsterdam for Poland via Westerbork. The German Jews who saw their compatriots off never forgave the Jewish Council and vowed that henceforth it would have no say at Westerbork. That vow they kept.

It was not long before the Dutch Jews learned the meaning of that resolve. On entering the camp, they quickly added a new German word to their vocabulary: *Schadenfreude*, which is the malicious pleasure people derive from other people's misfortunes. The German Jews behind the registration tables actually seemed glad to have the Dutch Jews. And although these former German citizens were known to extend equally perverse welcomes to other, non-Dutch, latecomers, including their own nationals, it was for the Dutch Jews that they displayed the greatest contempt. Identifying themselves, as it were, with the German victory over Holland, the camp's first "settlers" seemed to think that their former country's military superiority entitled them, by a natural devolution, to lord it over other Jews. On this pernicious assumption, the German Jew who seized the seat of a Dutch Jew who had momentarily left it to greet an acquaintance apparently felt well within his rights. "The Dutchman: 'Pardon me, sir, this seat is occupied.' The German: 'Occupied, occupied, who is actually occupied, the German or the Dutchman?' "

Mechanicus, who recorded this ludicrous scene, does not give the Dutchman's response, though we may safely assume that it was not insulting, because a wrong word, a false step, could bring not only the offender but an entire family to ruin. It happened, as we have seen, to Dr. Cohen and his wife. It happened to Holland's premier football announcer, Han Hollander. And it almost happened to Mechanicus himself. Forgetting for an instant where he was and to whom he was speaking, he made the mistake of calling a German Jew a *Kraut*. Wisely, he apologized and—*mirabile dictu*—found forgiveness.

So great was the tension between Dutch and German Jews that Mechanicus fully expected the two camps to come to blows, predicting "murder and slaughter" at the war's end. Mussolini's fall in the summer of 1943 seemed to bring that day infinitely closer. However, the apparent collapse of Italy left the German Jew strangely depressed. Inadvertently his mind drifted back to the prewar years. He remembered himself cursed in Germany, scorned or pitied by strangers, faceless and forsaken. The prospect of returning to such a life—stateless, homeless, unwanted—filled him with dread. Around him he caught the rumblings of revenge, communicated in the ominous metaphor of "a day of the ax," a rolling of heads on the day of judgment. Of a sudden, he was gripped by a desire to make amends, expediency sweeping sincerity before it.

To clear the air between themselves and the Dutch Jews, who now outnumbered them 6,000 to 4,000, the German Jews proposed the formation of an arbitration committee composed of an equal number of representatives from both sides, and invited Mechanicus to be the chairman. But the peace initiative never passed the embryo stage. After a few months of desultory negotiations, it simply collapsed under the burden of accumulated hatreds. Nor, it turned out, need the German Jews have bothered to make the effort. Eventually, as the "transport material" dried up, the German Jews were chivvied onto the train just like their predecessors—though many were shipped to camps where the living conditions were not so abysmally hopeless as to preclude survival altogether—and only one hundred of the Commandant's favorite Jews were present to witness Westerbork's liberation.

The unbending antagonism that kept German and Dutch Jews at daggers drawn had a solid basis in fact. Yet the fire could never have blazed so had not another element been fanning the flames all along. That element was fear. Fear forced a revolution in the conventional patterns of behavior, and Jews ended by discarding the wrap of civilization like so much excess baggage, as ships jettison cargo in a last-ditch effort to keep from going down.

Few things revealed this declining standard more sharply than the virtual extinction of privacy. Of all the hardships not connected with the transports, the lack of personal space was accounted the most difficult to endure by far. What with thousands of people privy to one's every move, one never had a moment to oneself. A woman dying of cancer in the washhouse by herself at least died alone, wrote Esther Hillesum. That having privacy during the act dying should strike her as worthy of being noted speaks for itself. So intense was this craving for solitude, for peace and quiet, that the inmates greeted a camp order forbidding singing and talking while shelling peas with a flood of applications for the task.

Disoriented as flies trapped in a jar, the prisoners blew up at the slightest provocation, scattering their rage in every direction. The Orthodox lambasted the youths who dared smoke on the sabbath; the youths, in turn, put down the orthodox for not washing. Veritable battles erupted around the stove, where an army of squatters regularly encamped to soak up the heat while others snaked and stumbled among them juggling potatoes, bread and vegetables for frying, toasting, and boiling. And even when there was no ostensible cause for aggravation, a pretext was as near as a pair of shoes sticking out harmlessly from under a bed, a box that was not in anybody's way, or a newspaper not folded "right."

Not many of the inmates could have mourned the passing of privacy more than Mechanicus. Thoughtful and introspective, he sadly diagnosed his own capitulation to the "dulling effect" of communal life he had detected in others. He no longer had the energy or the desire to write. He also was more selfish than before. When he found a "hiding place" where he could be alone for a few hours, he took care not to reveal it to anyone. "Man is like that," he rationalized. "He needs to withdraw from the filth and nastiness, from the chattering and the ravings of the masses."

As with privacy, so with private property. Because private ownership had become functionally impossible, it no longer commanded respect. People stole without shame or restraint—and called it "organizing." Socks, underwear, a spoon, an apple left for St. Nicholas—nothing was safe or sacred. A flourishing private sector economy arose on spoils "organized" from the tailoring and shoe repair shops. Routinely articles vanished from incoming parcels, thought never more routinely than after Nazi agents took over the "censorship" duties from Jews. Tobacco products ordinarily stood the least chance of getting by the "censor," for these valuable commodities could be bartered for other things, mostly food.

Never plentiful and sometimes scarce, food naturally topped the list of theft-worthy items, and kitchen work, with its almost unlimited opportunity for pilfering, was much sought after on that account alone. Though stealing food when hungry, Mechanicus conceded, could hardly be called theft (he had done it himself), he still thought the inmates guilty of a surplus of greed, as they invariably took more than they needed.

Nor was it just food and tobacco—objects—that were targeted for theft. So were affections. Infidelity was widespread and finished off many a marriage. The fact that it was impossible to live as husband and wife, except in the "little houses," no doubt played a role in turning Westerbork into a matrimonial graveyard. Far more destructive, however, was the prevailing anomie and concomitant sexual license. Westerbork's rampant sexuality struck more than one observer as unusually pervasive. H. O. E. Wohl, the Aryan officer who filed a report on Westerbork, wrote to his superiors that the "erotic atmosphere" in the camp was "extraordinary," a finding Dr. Cohen seconded. Mechanicus noted that the camp was full of pregnant women.

Few things more conclusively demonstrate that Westerbork bore little or no resemblance to annihilation camps than its aura of sexual promiscuity. Whereas a place like Auschwitz rapidly eliminated all thoughts of and desire for sex, in Westerbork both grew more intense, as though people, sensing their extinction, sought to maximize their pleasure while they still could. Pretty young women walked a minefield of innuendo and obscene jokes the moment they ventured out of doors. Mechanicus thought it revolting, the lewd dancing he witnessed in the bathroom during a visit to the punishment block. Barrack 21, which had been turned over to the unmarried adults, was the scene of unbridled sex. People coupled without shame, everywhere, and in full view of minors. "You have to be careful," observed Mechanicus, "not to let yourself be contaminated by the public sex life that goes on in all nooks and corners. Human beings here have sunk to the level of animals."

It would be difficult, apart from the death camps themselves, to think of a more gruesome place for children. Yet children came, stayed, and went, just like the adults. Impressed into the same "war of nerves," they suffered as much if not more. Their frustrations were legion, though no one can really know what they actually went through. Cooped up, with no place of their own (children stayed on the women's side of the barracks), they simply ran amok, cursed and detested. Parents lacked the will to enforce their authority. Always underfoot, always among adults, the children grew up much too fast, leaving them confused and bewildered.

There were schools for children, even a nursery and, from September, 1943, a small playground, with seesaws, horizontal bars, swings, and a sandpit. But there was no permanency to their lives. Overnight classmates, friends, and teachers disappeared, as if they had never existed. And what fears and anxieties Westerbork evoked in them! One girl, wrote Mechanicus, dreamt that her doll had to go on transport; another was threatened by her mother with a solo ride to Poland if she did not eat her pudding.

Westerbork's child specialists had their hands full, diagnosing case after case of bedwetting, assorted nervous disorders, and hypertension. Young boys and girls stopped growing. Babies did not thrive; because, surmised Mechanicus, their mothers, worried sick, could not produce milk of adequate quantity and quality. It has been estimated that in the summer of 1943 a child died every day.

Occasionally the Commandant would send the children out to work. In July of 1943 he ordered them to the moor to pick lupins. The sun was broiling and a number of them returned to the camp with severe sunstroke. Commandeered a month later to dig up potatoes at nearby farms, many came back ill from overexertion.

Yet it was said that the Commandant liked children. At the 1942 Hanukkah celebrations he was reported to have been moved by their singing. Eight months later they sang for him again, in German and in Hebrew, when he officiated at the opening ceremonies of an exhibition showcasing their toys. The children had made these toys themselves and some of them were shown in the film *Westerbork,* including a row of stuffed dogs. The director had thought of a cute ending to this scene: ominously, the first dog, an unseen force striking it, collapsed into the one next to it, setting off a chain reaction that brought down the entire display.

As every day seemed to bring some new, unexpected calamity, life in Westerbork was like that scene in the film. Regulations, orders, and directives followed one another with numbing frequency, keeping everybody on tenterhooks. There was teasing and tormenting in things large and small. Now frying or roasting for private use in the Central Kitchen was forbidden. Then all personal documents had to be surrendered. Now one *Sperre* "smashed," then another. Today you were allowed to send Rosh Hashanah greetings to relatives on the outside; tomorrow you could be sent out to help the Germans round up those very relatives.

It frightened Mechanicus to see how quickly people fell apart under these conditions. Strong men and women grew meek and timorous in a matter of days. Jews caught hiding eagerly supplied their captors with the names and addresses of their former hosts. Prisoners overnight lost the will to live. It was a rare individual who did not shed part of his former self in Westerbork.

Neither was Mechanicus altogether free from the dissipating effects of camp life. The longer he remained in Westerbork, he noted, the less he cared for his fellowman and the more he grew to dislike himself. After a year of camp life he confessed that he was well on the way to becoming a misanthrope. What horrified him most about the collective "mental degeneration" he saw around him was the stunting of the faculty for sympathy and affection, the callous indifference to the sufferings of others, and in writing of it, the diarist also gave the reason:

> It is hard to keep any feeling of sympathy. . . . Why should we feel sympathy towards Jews who go to Poland, towards two old folks helplessly facing their destiny? What does it matter—two people more or less, ten, a hundred, a thousand, or ten thousand Jews? Man has become powerless in the face of the all-prevailing wretchedness. The misfortunes of one individual in normal times affect him more than the combined distress of millions in time of war and revolution. He has to throw off all soft-heartedness with regard to himself in order to hold out and he cannot indulge in any soft-heartedness towards other people without damaging his morale. Life and death play no part any more. Anyone who is cut down by the storm is simply cut down. The man who defies the storm and stays alive is lucky if he manages to hang on to life.

Yet life went on. In spring the lupins bloomed and left the heath a blaze of purple. People pinned the flower to their clothing and in every barrack it was seen sticking out of makeshift vases. On hot summer days prisoners lay out in the "dunes," the piled up dirt and soil next to the trench, soaking up the sun. On warm evenings they sat around in undershirts and summer dresses chatting and playing games or watched loving couples stroll hand in hand down Boulevard des Misères.

Year-round there were concerts and sports events, chess and bridge tournaments, though these were rarely completed. Friday nights and Saturday mornings the barracks echoed with prayer and singing. You could go to the barber and get a shave and a haircut. You could go to the "store" and get a tube of toothpaste. Men congratulated each other on the cut of their suits. Women draped in furs challenged Westerbork's mud in high heels. People went visiting. They read the newspapers and argued the contents. Women gave birth. Boys were Barmitzvahed. People married and people died.

In Westerbork there were rules for everything but few that could not be broken. Discipline was lax. Resourceful inmates always seemed to find ways around the curfew (usually set for the hours between 8:00 p.m. and 6:00 a.m.). Nor did the threat of punishment keep prisoners from marching right up to the train to say their final goodbyes to friends and loved ones. No one was allowed to speak to the S-detainees, but few heeded the injunction. Food and cigarettes somehow managed to reach jailed inmates, despite the order banning all outsiders from the premises. There was no smoking in the barracks, so many smoked clandestinely in the bathrooms. Though rules concerning cleanliness abounded, the barracks were rarely clean. It was only when high-ranking Nazis came visiting or when the Commandant had one of his periodic seizures for *Ordnung* that the inmates were set upon to apply spit and polish.

Corporal punishment was practically unknown. Generally punishments were so mild that anything above a certain acceptable minimum inspired not fear but indignation. One time this happened after an escape involving two men from Mechanicus' barrack. All of Westerbork was enraged when the Commandant's understudy, a Dutchman named Van Dam, attempted to learn what the other male occupants of barrack 71 knew of this escape by making them do "nursery gymnastics"—standing up, lying down, jogging—for three consecutive days. Previously the reaction had been equally vehement when this same Van Dam had ordered the men from the S-barrack to roll in the mud because one of them had been slow in doffing his cap in his presence. Indignation turned to glee, however, when a badly mauled Van Dam was seen limping through the compound. Drunk, he had smashed the Commandant's car into a tree. A small measure of justice seemed to have been done.

The regimen at the work place was no more stringent. The Statistical Office prepared countless graphs, tables, and charts measuring camp productivity. It always recorded or projected stupendous production figures. The film *Westerbork* depicted a dedicated work force reveling in the joys of labor. But in reality output was small, in spite of the best efforts of group leaders to get the most out of their charges. Group leaders could be deported for not meeting their production quotas.

Mechanicus' experience was typical. In October, 1943, complying with a new directive requiring everyone to work, he reported to Barrack 78 to shell peas and beans. He showed up punctually at eight, only to be told to come back in the afternoon. In the afternoon, he was instructed to come back in the morning. Two days later he was "laid off."

At the beginning of December the diarist was given a new assignment—foil sorting, a job the Germans considered important for the war effort. It consisted of removing silver foil from the condensers of stolen Philips radios.

The workday in Barrack 57, the foil-sorting unit, was divided into a morning and afternoon shift. Mechanicus worked the latter. His first day on the job, December 6, passed pleasantly enough. The only sign of industry was the steady patter of the men and women facing each other across a long row of adjoining tables. No sooner had they learned that the author of a book on Russia was among them than groups of workers left their work stations. Curious to know more about the Soviet experiment, they clustered around him and showered him with questions.

Perhaps it was to eliminate the cause of disruption by co-opting it that Mechanicus was made supervisor, over his own strenuous objections, before the day was done. Assigned to the morning shift, he never came to work on time, deliberately setting a bad example. The foil sorters under him quickly followed suit and were in no rush to get their hands dirty when they finally did show up for work. At first they simply hovered around the stove waiting for their pieces of bread to turn the proper shade of brown so they could eat. But they never sat down for very long. There was gossip to swap, jokes to tell, rumors to spread. Later in the day they sang and prayed and read the newspapers, doing full justice to the unit's unofficial motto: "Be idle but do it well and systematically—it is for a good cause!"

The "good cause" was to contribute as little as possible to the German war machine—which was easier said than done. By working hard you might prolong your stay but also the war; by slacking off you might shorten the war but also your stay. Weighing one against the other was no simple matter. To their credit, most Jews seemed to have opted for the latter rather than the former, the threat of deportation notwithstanding. An order issued in December, 1943, forbidding prayer during work hours was honored only in the breach. The campaign against "work-shy" women, launched by the Commandant at about the same time, was also stillborn. Many of these so-called shirkers were far too busy with their own small "businesses"—ironing, altering, tailoring, cleaning, mostly for the wives of the camp's elite—to bother responding to the call. Nor did the appointment of a female whip-hand to assist Mechanicus stop the workers from flushing part of their daily output down the toilet.

The lack of productivity was a foremost concern of the camp's labor leaders. Alternating between the carrot and the stick, they pulled out all the stops to bring the workers to heel. The group leader of the camp's bookkeeping and purchasing section preferred using threats:

> In an extremely sharply worded talk with Herr Todt-mann [the Commandant's Jewish Secretary] the *Ober-sturmführer* has complained that the discipline and the work output in the camp leave much to be desired. He expressly told Herr Todtmann to convey this information to the administrative leaders. . . . As far as discipline is concerned, the current situation will no longer

be tolerated. It is not permitted that you go for a stroll during work hours, stand around conversing in the streets, or go to the doctor. The O.D. has been notified to report every infraction immediately. The O.D. has the same police powers as the police in the occupied countries. You must also show complete obedience to the Group Leaders. All resistance must be immediately reported, inasmuch as the Group Leader will otherwise be subject to disciplinary action.

If we ourselves do not immediately act upon these problems, the character of the camp will change. It is up to every individual to do his part. . . . In addition, I might mention that if the work is scheduled to start at 7:30 in our group, *everyone* has to be present at that time.

The shoddy work of the foil-sorters of Mechanicus' unit did not go unnoticed for long. On December 21 the Controller came visiting to remind the sorters of the potential consequences of their idleness. Bleating an old refrain, he informed them that the Bureau of Non-Ferrous Metals in the Hague, which kept track of such things, was most unhappy with their performance. If there was no significant improvement, he warned, they would not only have their hours lengthened, but also jeopardize any chance of Westerbork becoming a labor camp with about four thousand to five thousand permanent residents.

Turning a deaf ear to all such threats, Mechanicus was content to sit back and relax, letting the workers shift as they saw fit. That was too much for one inspector. Surveying the scene of sloth, he complained loudly, and, after trading insults, left with a promise to have Mechanicus removed from his post. Within days the latter was back at his old work station. He fetched tea from the Central Kitchen, tea and newspapers. Finally, in February, 1944, he managed to secure a note from a friendly doctor stating that he was unable to work, once more leaving him free to do as he pleased.

Clearly, neither the regime nor the regimen at Westerbork was so abusive that it left the inmate without any sense of his former self. He kept his name, his hair, and his own clothes. Though a prisoner, he never developed what Dr. Ottenstein called a "prisoner psychosis"; in other words, he never became fully resigned to his prisoner status. (The only group of inmates to which such a psychosis might be fitted were those who had spent year after year in the camp, to wit, the Long-Term Residents.) If there was a discernible mood, it was that of a "general depression," as Herr Wohl would note, which is not the same, however, as a "prisoner psychosis."

What is more, the prisoner was not without hope. After mid-1943, he fully expected the war to end soon. And just as he thought to have time on his side—yet another week and the war might be history—so he latched on to every rumor that carried a promise, however faint, of his delivery.

Not surprisingly, most of these rumors were grounded in the notion that the transports would soon cease because, with the tide of war having turned against her, Germany would need all the trains she could muster.

A former inmate, H. N. Andriesse, repeated what another inmate had told him concerning these rumors. "I have already seen eighteen transports arrive, and all eighteen times have the English landed in France and has Sweden declared war on Germany, and all eighteen times it was said that there would no longer be any trains leaving from Westerbork, and despite all that the deportations have continued without letup."

Rumors came and went like the mist on the moor. Now Westerbork was to become a labor camp, then a military hospital for the Germans. In July and August of 1943 there was great rejoicing following the Allied landing in Sicily and the subsequent fall of Mussolini. Many then believed that it was only a matter of time before their relatives and friends would be coming back from Poland. When that same August a rumor flew that Hitler had resigned and Goering had taken over, a wave of excitement surged through the camp, followed by the inevitable letdown. Spirits sank even lower two months later with the "news" that Russia and Germany were negotiating a separate peace.

And thus the inmates watched for every telltale sign of Germany's impending defeat. They read the newspapers and scanned the skies. In the fall and winter of 1943 squadrons of British and American planes began plowing the skies over Westerbork on bombing missions to German cities, and each time, reports Mechanicus, the inmates went "wild with joy." In late November, some of these planes were shot down and ten captured American airmen were brought to Westerbork for medical observation and treatment. The inmates gave them a hero's welcome.

Rumors also sprouted about the unknown. Though no one had much illusion about Poland, figuring that life would be hard there, the attitude toward Theresienstadt, by contrast, was inexplicably sanguine. The fact that those earmarked for the *Musterlager* often left Westerbork in third-class carriages no doubt helped buttress it. Life was said to be good in Theresienstadt. Opinion had it that in this quaint garrison town there was no barbed wire, plenty of food, and hot and cold running water. Many of the Theresienstadt-bound inmates actually came to view their trip as a pleasure outing—as if they were going to the Isle of Wight or Capri, says Mechanicus. "How credulous man is," he wrote in disbelief, "how naive and ready to imagine that the place where he does not happen to be is better than the place where he is, at present, relatively speaking, quite well off."

But Mechanicus, skeptic though he was, was not immune from self-delusion himself. In July, 1943, a "telepathic friend" told him that that the war would be over by August 16. During the next few weeks Mechanicus frequently alluded to his friend's forecast. And when August 16 came and the war was still on, he made a special point of mentioning the failed prediction in his diary.

The belief, in the summer of 1943, that the war could not go on much longer was widespread; this belief, combined with the tolerable living conditions at Westerbork—those who had been at Vught and Amersfoort could vouch for that—probably kept more Jews from escaping. For escape was not difficult. Mechanicus toyed with the idea more than once, only to reject it on both practical and philosophical grounds. He could easily have escaped, for example, that time he escorted his sick brother to the camp's gate where a truck was waiting to take him back to Amsterdam. (His brother had multiple sclerosis and was married to an Aryan, hence his release.) Freedom beckoned, but the fear of jeopardizing his brother's safety held him back—that, and the belief that the war would be over soon.

But a more profound consideration kept him and others at the camp. Escaping Westerbork, one would be free only in relative terms—an ersatz freedom being all that was available to Jews beyond the barbed wire so long as the war continued. Thus many of the inmates, Mechanicus and Dr. Cohen contended, actually preferred sitting out the war in the camp to returning to the uncertainty of life on the outside. To be sure, there were the transports, but these at least were predictable and with a little bit of luck and effort might be evaded or, at the minimum, deferred. On the moor one did not live in constant fear of the *Razzias*, the pounding of boots and the knock on the door.

Here one was among Jews, with one's own. Here was a community, albeit a community of fate, a *Schicksalgemeinschaft*. And in this community there arose over time a special kind of in-house culture which kept spirits from breaking. Many a song was born in the work place or in the barracks. One such, "Westerbork Serenade," an ode to love, sang of a heart that "beat like the hammerblows in the airplane-stripping shop." In "The Most Beautiful Girls in the Lawa" [the camp 'store'], an imnate told of a love that was more beautiful even than the flowers in his prewar garden. A S-detainee averred in song that "nothing bothered him at all," and that "In Westerbork you have to be an optimist / That he who can last ten rounds / Won't get knocked out." And when the workers in the airplane-stripping plant began to sing, wrote yet another versifier, "The nuts and bolts just happen to fall off all by themselves."

Irony, sarcasm, and mild forms of self-ridicule—in short, gallows humor—were the spiritual defenses Jews reflexively raised against their awful fate. To get Gemmeker's goat and to warn others of his approach, they would shout "Achtung!" upon his arrival. When in June of 1943 Jews from mixed marriages were confronted with the sterilization dilemma, the following grim joke made the rounds: What is the comparative of *ster* (*ster*, Dutch for *star*)—ster, sterile, ster-off.

The rumor mill was dubbed the JPA, the Jewish Press Agency. "Transport contest" was another name for the camp's track and field competitions, since a winning performance might result in a stay of deportation. Some referred to Westerbork as Westerbork-le-Bain, in view of the many amenities. Cynics registered their skepticism when they dismissed the "exchange projects" as an *Austauschwitz, Austausch* being the German word for exchange and *Witz* that for witticism or joke, thus "exchange joke." In other words, they thought that those who applied to go to a special camp for a possible exchange with German nationals in Allied hands would ultimately wind up in Auschwitz anyway. Because of their habit of monopolizing the space around the stove, making access difficult or impossible, people referred to the Turkish Jews as the "Dardanelles."

The inmates also developed a special language, a kind of shorthand conceptualizing of a whole range of autochthonous phenomena. "Vitamin C" stood for connections—very important in Westerbork for getting things done. The baptized Jews lived in *Schmattenau* (Barrack 73), from the Yiddish word for convert, *Geschmatte*. The *Chateaux rouges* referred to the brick outdoor toilets, so christened by the *Barnevelders*. Thieving, as we know, went by the name of "organizing;" the initials *M.S.W.* for *Macht sich wichtig*, was said of someone who acted self-important, like a big shot. Westerbork's main street was the Boulevard des Misères, or, alternately, *rachmones* or *tsorres allee*, that is, street of woe, both from Hebrew.

The Emergency Squad, the auxiliary Jewish police force known in the German as *Notbereitschaft* and abbreviated NB, was dubbed the Nebbich Brigade, which roughly translates as "losers' brigade." An "embryo case" (E-case) was a person whose exemption request was being processed by the Applications Office, hence to be kept off the transport list as long as possible. A much-quoted phrase from one of the cabarets was *Hunde sind glückliche Geschöpfe*—Dogs are lucky—this in contrast to the Jews. To beat somebody up was to beat him or her "transport-ready." When someone shouted "Eighteen" it was meant as a warning, that number playing a similar role in the card game of *Skat* of *Tarok*.

Space and time," wrote Mechanicus in the summer of 1943 "have ceased to exist—man lives against a background of nothingness." Against such a background, he added, life proceeds as in a film, a film that is both "horrible" and "enthralling," requiring the actor—in this case, himself—"to clench his teeth as he played his part."

What Mechanicus felt—the sense of experience being flattened to an unreality—later was given the name "acute depersonalization." It was the mind's way of coping with a reality that, at bottom, was frightening and sordid in the extreme. Mechanicus, however, was fortunate. He had the sensibility to find Westerbork, "enthralling" despite everything. He also had courage. When his turn came to go we may assume that he packed his belongings, pushed them over to the train in a wheel-barrow, and took his place in the cattle car with the same stoicism he had displayed on previous occasions. In the final analysis, the diarist observed, everything depends on oneself, on one's capacity for transcending the squalor of existence. "The things in life," he wrote on July 29, 1943,

> are as dramatic or tragic as you yourself want to make them. . . . Captivity means the barbed wire fence and the discipline of hut life, but with a little imagination and a sense of humor and a love of nature you can create a world of your own in which it is possible to forget the captivity of the material body. Both in your working hours, provided they are spent out of doors and do not go beyond your normal strength—something which does not happen at Westerbork—and also in your free hours which you can spend outside, you can enjoy the vastness of the sky and the moor and the birds. The sky is so delightful here and there is color on the moor. The sunsets are enchanting. Flocks of seagulls with white bodies and black heads, perhaps a thousand of them together, spend their lives cavorting in the air. I can stand and look at the gulls for long periods on end—they are the symbol of true freedom."

4

Etty

TRANSPORT

By means of graphs and tables (trick shots) a short history of the camp is presented. Formerly a camp established by the Dutch government as an assembly point for Jews. July 1942: takeover of the camp by the SD
[Sicherheitsdienst—*Security Police*].
Carrying out of transports for labor supply to the East, later to Vught, Theresienstadt, Bergen-Belsen, Vitelles, etc. Shots of incoming and outgoing transports; registration in Big Barrack; bustle at the train,
Ordedienst—*police cordon, Flying Column, sick transport(?)*

From the film script of *Westerbork*

In Westerbork for a brief time there was a young woman of twenty-nine, Esther Hillesum. Etty, as she was called by her friends, came from a middle-class, cultured home. She was known for her vivacity, her warm spontaneity. She was bright, curious, and sensitive. But after seeing Westerbork she realized that she could never again be the same. Westerbork provoked her as an enigma, something unfathomable, impenetrable. Above all, she was bewildered, grappling with the mysteries of which mankind has never been quit—the mystery of suffering, the mystery of innocence, the mystery of love. In examining these questions a revolution was made in her being. She looked into her soul and beyond. It compelled her to bear witness. It drove her to set down what she called "a piece of Jewish history on the heath of Drente."

Among her writings about Westerbork are two long letters—essays, really—each a dozen pages or so. These were printed, while she was still alive, in Holland's underground press. Others have written about Westerbork in far greater volume. But these two letters of Esther Hillesum do more than analyze or depict. They are cameos on which small details stand out boldly. They are a transparency through which is visible the shape of a soul.

Esther Hillesum came from a home where the cultivation of the mind was a consuming pursuit. Her grandfather had been chief rabbi of Holland's three northern provinces. Her father, a calm, benign man, impractical as only the bookish can be, was professor of classical studies and the rector of a secondary school. One brother, Mischa, was a gifted pianist; another practiced medicine. Etty herself had obtained a doctorate in jurisprudence, though her intellectual interest delved deeply into the fields of literature, languages, religion, psychology, and the arts.

In her home and school she had been nurtured in a bourgeois idealism of a particular high-minded sort which subscribes to the belief that by following his better mind, man will be made perfect. This brand of idealism was severely tested in the camp. Etty saw people being hunted, collected, and put on trains that conveyed them to oblivion. But as she saw here a mystery of suffering so in her heart she discovered a mystery of love. What the Jew Paul wrote concerning charity, the charity that "suffereth long, the charity that is greater than either faith or hope," she laid as a balm to her heart. "It's not merely enough to save oneself physically," she wrote. "It's a matter of how one has kept oneself alive." The suffering that the Jews of Holland and elsewhere were experiencing at the hands of the Germans would be valueless, she believed, if it did not also carry to the world proof that charity and love were the only pillars on which mankind could build.

Etty was among the first Dutch Jews to become acquainted with Westerbork. Up until August, 1942, when she first saw the camp, she had been unaware that for some time a few hundred stateless German Jews had been living there. Astonished, Etty met people with memories of Dachau and Buchenwald, with stories of the *St. Louis* and its fruitless quest of a landing. She beheld a village of barracks where four years earlier, an old "pioneer" told her proudly, "not a speck of life, not a little flower, not even a worm," had been evident. In Westerbork she blamed her neglect. With wry self-condemnation she explained that she had been too busy during these years "taking up collections for the little Chinese and Spanish children." With honest shame she acknowledged to herself how far she had fallen short of sharing the "Jewish Schicksal" which had been unfolding in Germany for nearly a decade.

She could easily have gone into hiding. She had a wealth of offers. But she dismissed them all, even when as a social worker for the Jewish Council her duties enabled her to come in and out of the camp almost at will. The pressing appeals from her friends were of no avail. She refused to evade the "Jewish fate" on the principle that she would not profit from her privilege as an intellectual while the large Jewish proletariat had no such escape. It was her duty, as she saw it, to be with the victims, to share their pain, to be of use to them.

Westerbork filled Etty with horror. What she must have felt in Auschwitz we shall never know. One suspects that in her, a sensitive plant nurtured in a loving atmosphere, the conviction was born that from the evil at hand some great truth might be drawn down. If she discovered this truth, it accompanied her into the Auschwitz gas chamber.

Paradoxically, though Westerbork horrified her, Etty also "loved" it. Whenever her functions with the Jewish Council required her to be away from the camp for any length of time, she experienced a feeling of nostalgia, of loss, and could hardly wait to be back. The two months she had spent at Westerbork, Etty recorded in her diary during a brief stay in Amsterdam in mid-September of 1942, had been "the richest" months of her life. The camp added a new dimension to Etty's life, one she had hitherto only read about in books—St. Augustine, Tolstoy, Rilke—and had always wanted to experience for herself: the suffering that purifies and makes whole. For Etty life often had a way of imitating art.

The business on which Etty had come to Amsterdam was personal rather than official. It was to be with her lover, Julius Spier, who lay dying in Amsterdam. Drawing on connections in the Jewish Council, Etty had obtained permission to spend a few days in the city. While she was there, he died. It was the first time Etty had seen a dead person, and now she knew for a fact what she had only intuited before—that death was not to be feared, that it enhanced life's beauty and meaning.

Julius Spier, a Jewish refugee from Nazi Germany, played a key role in Etty's development. He was a catalyst in a process of self-discovery that presumably ended only with her death. He encouraged her to write and taught her to cope with her neuroses, manifested in frequent and prolonged headaches, depressions, spells of nausea, and assorted stomach ailments. It was largely because of him that she considered the war years to have been the best years of her life, the most decisive, the most meaningful, the most beautiful. Friends noticed the change. They said she had never been more radiant.

They had met in the first months of 1941. He was fifty-four and she twenty-seven. He was a psychochirologist, that is, he read palms for clues to the personality, and he had studied under Jung. Prior to that, he had variously been a banker, publisher, and an aspiring singer. Etty pronounced him a "magical personality."

Compared to Spier, Etty was a mere child. At age twenty-seven, though no longer in school, she was still living like a student. Apart from giving a few Russian lessons, she did not work. She was boarding in a middle-class home in Amsterdam, and passed her days pleasantly enough, considering it was wartime. She went bicycling, attended concerts, took walks with Spier, had therapy, or sat at the "most beautiful place on earth"—her desk—reading or working on her Russian. Mostly though, she read, devouring Tolstoy and Dostoevsky and swooning over Rilke. By her own admission, she was 'spoilt.'

Shortly after Etty began going to Spier for therapy, she started a diary. Parts of that diary, which she kept during 1941 and 1942, were published in Holland in 1981 with the title *Het verstoorde leven,* and in English, two years later, as *An Interrupted Life.* Also published during this time were some letters written by Etty from Westerbork, a slim volume that includes the two letters previously published by the Dutch underground. As title for this collection the publisher fittingly chose Esther's own self-descriptive phrase, *Het denkende hart van de barak* ("The Thinking Heart of the Barrack"). Together, the diaries and the letters, but especially the diaries, tell the story of the last years of Etty's life, climaxed literarily and spiritually with the "two letters from Westerbork," her best, that is to say, her most mature, most powerful work.

Etty was unique. At a time when Jews hated Germans and considered them brutes, Etty continued to think of them as people. Thus she did not fear them. Whenever, an early diary entry related, she caught herself hating Germans, even wishing their total destruction, she always felt "terribly ashamed and deeply unhappy." For it was not necessary for people to be good in order to love them. Hating was cheap and morally indefensible, and "every atom of hate added to the world," she wrote in her "first" letter from Westerbork, "only makes it more inhospitable than it already is."

The worst thing about hating, Etty maintained, was that it kept Jews from realizing that the Germans could not really hurt them. It was only because they *felt* "persecuted, humiliated, and oppressed," only because they had a weak inner life, because they hated, Etty wrote prior to the mass deportations from Westerbork, that they viewed the German measures against them as if they were death sentences. To Etty, having a curfew, being banned from certain beaches, not being able to ride the streetcar, were only minor vexations when compared with the infinite possibilities we carry within us. If one had a rich inner life, it probably did not make much difference whether one was inside a camp or outside of one, Etty said.

Everywhere she looked Etty saw beauty and God's hand. There was not a single thing in the world that did not belong, and one thing was as crucial to it as the next. A poem by Rilke was as "real and important" to Etty "as a young man falling out of a plane." The horror of war did not make the sky less magnificent or the jasmine less fragrant. Beautiful dreams could "exist side by side with the most horrible reality." Spier was no less real than Hitler.

Less spiritual, many of Etty's companions could not understand why their friend would not go into hiding or show so little rancor toward Germans. Gently rebuking her, they told her she was "unworldly," mystical, resigned, and naive. A doctor said she was too intense, too spiritual, that she lived too much inside herself, and advised her to go out and enjoy herself more.

Etty disagreed with both her friends and the doctor. She could not see why others considered her mysticism harmful, since she had come to it only after first having "stripped things down to their naked reality." She knew very well that the world was collapsing, and said she welcomed the challenge of allowing herself to become a battlefield. To her that was living fully, inwardly and outwardly.

What she was trying to do, Etty explained, was to look at things historically, sub specie aeternitatis, taking the long as well as the short view. There had always been suffering and always would be. Each century merely invented new ways to inflict it. But what really mattered was the quality of our emotions. In other words, the fact that Jews wore yellow stars, were put in concentration camps, and sent to their death was less important than the manner in which they responded to these torments. That attitude was not one of resignation, she insisted, because "moral certainty and moral indignation are also part of the big emotions."

For all her presumed 'unworldliness' and lack of realism, it is a fact that Etty grasped what the Nazis had in store for Jews long before most others. Two weeks prior to the first official transport from Holland to the East, Etty realized that they were after the Jews' "total destruction," and that "total destruction" must needs include her. It was a new insight and one for which she was prepared to make room. People feared death unnecessarily, she said. A few days more or less made no difference, for every day could be a lifetime in itself.

Before coming to Westerbork, Etty spent several weeks working in the offices of the Jewish Council in Amsterdam as a Cultural Worker. Her appointment coincided with the beginning of the mass deportations from Holland. Until then, the war had hardly touched her.

It proved to be a great shock, suddenly coming face to face with a humanity straining every muscle to preserve life. She thought it vulgar and even balked at her assignments. Every free moment she was off in a corner, reading Rilke.

In Westerbork, this Etty was no longer. There nothing was too much for her. Saintly in her selflessness, a boundless compassion drove her. With a leather bag slung over her shoulder, in a drab raincoat, she dashed from barrack to barrack to bring a ray of warmth and kindliness. A fellow inmate recalled that an age-old wisdom, a thousand-year-old morning seemed to have settled on her young, radiant face. In the camp of the doomed she became what she had hoped to become—"a balm on many wounds."

In the second letter published in the Dutch underground press, the letter of August, 1943, Etty described the day before a transport and the morning of the train's departure for Poland. The transport she wrote about occurred on Tuesday the 24th. After seeing it, Esther seriously doubted whether she would ever again laugh or be merry. Almost half the deportees were elderly and sick, another third S-detainees. It also contained fifty Jews whose names had not originally been cast for Poland. These had been added at the last moment to teach the Jews a lesson in collective responsibility. A boy in blue pajamas had hidden himself in a tent to avoid the transport. Other Jews, fearing reprisals, had gone after him and quickly brought him back. But the Commandant had exacted fifty fresh victims none the less, and now everyone was blaming the "escapee" and not the Commandant. "That boy," predicted Etty, "would have a difficult time of it" on the train to Poland.

The Commandant reportedly was in a foul mood. The night before Allied planes had been very much in evidence, and a nearby town had been hit. In the Jews, however, the buzzing and bombing briefly rekindled, as it did before every transport, the "infantile hope" that bombs would destroy the tracks and prevent the train from leaving.

To make her observations on that summer morning Etty had concealed herself in a barrack directly across from the train. By occupying this vantage point she had violated Camp Order No. 8, which allowed no unauthorized person to leave their assigned quarters on the morning of a transport. As was customary before a departure, curfew had gone into effect the previous evening an hour earlier than usual. All doors and windows of the barracks had been locked and no one not included or employed in the actual transport was permitted abroad. Hence that morning there would be no roll call and the workday began at 11 rather than the usual 7:30. Camp Order No. 8 ended on the macabre note that "the rest of the day will proceed as normal."

The train Esther was observing from her hiding place had been idling at the platform since 11 o'clock the previous morning, as if, in the acid phrase of one inmate, "the executioner had laid the ax before the eyes of the condemned." The train consisted of a drab row of discolored empty freight cars, with a passenger car for the escort staff in the rear. In some cars a few paper mattresses covered the floor; these were for the sick. A barrel stood in the center of each car, a bucket of sand next to it—the barrel was for the bodily functions, the sand served to cover the traces. Esther noticed how since its arrival the train had symbolically divided the camp into two parts.

As the early morning wore on, the paved road alongside the train gradually came alive. A companion of Etty's, the journalist Philip Mechanicus, had joined her. Etty heard someone near her saying wryly, "This has always been the grandstand to watch the transports." A few young children had also discovered their secret observatory; they pressed their noses against the tiny window. Together in the dusk of the barrack the quiet man, the serious young woman, and the chattering children watched the sick file by on stretchers. Esther saw a mortally ill man saying Sh'ma for himself. She saw a father blessing his wife and child and being blessed in return by an elderly rabbi "with a snow-white beard and the fiery profile of a prophet." A few young mothers, their infants on their laps, were seated at the entrance to the car, their legs dangling outside, and eagerly gulped the fresh air before the bolt on the door was inexorably shut.

The evening before Etty had been walking through the camp with Philip Mechanicus. The sky had been gray and overcast. Everywhere in this oppressive dusk people were grouped in small clusters. "Look," Mechanicus had remarked, "that is exactly how people stand around after a disaster when they gather on street corners to discuss it." And Etty had burst out, "But that is just what is so incomprehensible. It is still before the disaster."

And this morning the judgment which overtook Westerbork each Tuesday was fulfilling itself. Aghast, Etty noticed a sudden swarm of brutes in green uniforms carrying clubs and guns on the paved road. Mechanicus momentarily shivered; she understood his mumbled, "That's how they are, the bastards. That's how they look," as referring to his own experience of the Dutch Nazis in the punishment camp at Amersfoort. "When I think of the faces of the armed escorts in their green uniforms," Esther later wrote in her "transport" letter, "My God, those faces! . . . I have never been so terrified of anything than I was of those faces. I got all in a muddle with the words that form the motif of our existence. And God created man in his own image. That phrase spent a difficult morning with me."

When the train's twenty-seven cars were almost full, the most important Jewish leaders began arriving at the platform. The man with the "brow of a young scholar, and weary, very weary shoulders" was Dr. Ottenstein of the *Antragstelle*, the bureau which examined the claims for exemption from deportation. Some other time perhaps he might have been able to do something for the old woman who was brandishing "a batch of papers in his face," but not this time; after all, this was a "punishment transport." The Application Officer shook his head and turned away. Etty observed that his shoulders drooped even more than before.

The children were the first to spot the Commandant striding briskly past the train with his Jewish secretary. The *Obersturmführer's* face was "the color of steel" on account of that boy in blue pajamas and the planes, Etty surmised. His gestures conveyed that things weren't going fast enough for him. His Jewish amanuensis, however, stylishly dressed in "beige riding-breeches and a brown sports jacket," seemed bored and was killing time by romping with a beautiful brown hunting dog. Etty noted that Herr Todtmann had the "sporty but insipid look of the British club man," and their cavorting reminded her of a scene from an English society page.

Other ranking Jews appeared on the platform and gathered around the Commandant. "They want to look 'important' too," said someone close to Etty.

The train was set to depart.

Etty:

> The doors are closing; the mass of people are being squashed and pushed to the back of the freight cars. Through the tiny slits on top you see heads and hands, which later wave, when the train leaves. The Commandant rides once more past the entire train on a bicycle. He then makes a brief gesture with his hand, like a prince in an operetta. A little messenger boy rushes forward and respectfully takes his bicycle from him. The whistle makes a piercing noise. A train carrying one thousand Jews is leaving Holland.

The organization of the weekly, and sometimes twice-weekly, transports was met by the Nazi administrators with little of the diabolical ingenuity commensurate with the terminating point of the train. For the scenes which etched themselves on the mind of Esther Hillesum as she observed the bestowal of people into freight cars—the forlorn parade along the platform of hundreds of men, women, children, and nursing babies; the broken ranks of the ill; the mentally disturbed, and the elderly, along with the taunting faces of the brutes in green—these scenes formed the dangling tail of a long string of paperwork, an unbroken chain of written orders, forms, documents, and filing cards that wound unperceived through the nation at large. A small staff of clerks, secretaries, functionaries, and accountants was knotted at various points along the string, in Amsterdam and the Hague, in the provincial capitals, and in Westerbork itself. Inseparable from the wretchedly pathetic scene at the train platform of the camp was the dull, plodding application of this paper-pushing enterprise, presenting an aspect of placid industry that raised the transports to the work of abomination.

This paper empire was jointly operated by the German Central Office for Jewish Emigration and the Security Service, by German and Dutch Nazis as well as regular Dutch functionaries following regular Dutch orders, and the Jewish administrators in the Jewish Council and in Westerbork. Their labors achieved with the pen and the typewriter, with memos, directives, and indexes, the removal of more than 100,000 Jews in a period of twenty-six months.

Yet, paper is thin and the bureaucratic feat could not have been sustained had there not loomed behind the paper the shadow of the enforcer. This shadow had sprung alive at the commencement of the deportations. The lightning-quick raids on Jewish ghettos and quarters, called *Razzias*, netted thousands of people who were at once put on trains to Westerbork, many of them arriving in the camp still wearing their housecoats and slippers. Some even came in nothing more than their underwear.

One of the largest *Razzias* occurred on October 2, 1942, during the biggest transport month of all, when fifteen thousand Jews entered Westerbork and close to twelve thousand immediately went to Poland. An unknown Flying Column worker whose diaries have survived the war noted that their arrival at Westerbork "defie[d] all description. Thousands of people . . . arrived . . . from all parts of Holland. One part came on foot, others by bus, others again by train . . . Then came a second, a third, and a fourth transport from Amsterdam . . . Hopeless!"

The *Razzias* served to impress on the victims their ineluctable destiny and the implacable methods of the authorities, and they were so effective that except for an occasional *Grossrazzia*, the Jewish populace was cowed into following the paper route as the lesser evil. Rather than being swept off the streets and hauled away in trucks, they chose to abide by an "evacuation" that generally began with the arrival of a plain envelope bearing the imprint of the Jewish Council. "I regret to inform you that your name appears on this list of the Security Police," the enclosed letter would state, as well as where and when the addressee was to present himself, not omitting the order to shut off his water, gas, and electricity, and to turn over his keys to a local police official. Further instructions bore on bringing warm clothing and enough food for one day, all important papers such as birth certificates, bank statements, financial documents, ration and identity cards, and lastly the admonition not to bring unnecessary baggage, especially not books.

A similar type of letter, headed "CALLUP!" might arrive from the German Central Office for Jewish Emigration rather than the Jewish Council. Here there was no apologetic prelude, but a straightforward summons including an even more curtailed baggage list limited to the essentials of a three-day journey. A couple of sheets and blankets, a plate, spoon, and mug, a few pairs of socks and undershirts, one pair of overalls and work boots, and a pullover were to be packed in no more than one valise or rucksack with the name "Holland" in large clear lettering on it. This summons plainly stated that illness was no excuse for neglecting the order. The paper was particularly detailed in specifying the information to be supplied concerning finances, including savings, stocks, insurance policies, real estate, art objects, gold and silver valuables, jewelry, and so forth. A travel permit to Hooghalen, the hamlet nearest Westerbork, was enclosed. The German authorities granted the addressee the use of the streetcar or bus, otherwise prohibited to Jews, in order to convey himself to the train station.

When the "evacuees" arrived in Westerbork, either in the

middle of the night or in the early morning, they were immediately ushered into the Big Barrack. Here they were greeted by the volleying noise of typewriters situated on a dais which at other times served as the stageboards for the antics of the cabaret cast. Jewish inmates were waiting to register them; the men dressed in their best suits, the women in smart outfits, sat behind a phalanx of long tables. Past this official cadre the arrivals filed, being relieved at each table of some personal papers, losing at each stop some part of their former life. Lastly, they were handed over to a desk occupied by the agents of Lippmann Rosenthal, a company which despite its Jewish-sounding name was composed of Dutch Nazis working under the German *Devisenschutzkommando*. In Westerbork Lippman Rosenthal completed the registration process by unburdening the newcomers of their last possessions—money, jewelry, heirlooms, down to a fountain pen or even a stamp. Bodily searches were conducted, and one female agent was always present to frisk the women.

The registration procedure took place in a glaring brightness as if to impress upon the new arrivals that here nothing could be hidden. White tablecloths and doctors' and nurses' uniforms raised the brightness to a dazzling spectrum. In this pitiless light incoming Jews descried the prominent forms of their new lords, Schlesinger and Gemmeker. Schlesinger with his Hitler mustache and legs astride would be "exhorting the people being registered," one employee of the Jewish Council wrote, "to hurry up in a gruff, often rough tone of voice," every hesitation provoking his anger, while Gemmeker stood by quietly, "merely observing." After having been assigned by the Housing Office to their barracks, the new inmates were then led out into the darkness of the dismal camp.

Under the punctilious Commandant, Westerbork ran on schedule. The time of handling an incoming transport had been computed at two hours for every one hundred persons. The outgoing transports, however, required far more time. They not only took longer to complete, the trains for Poland also demanded a higher degree of organization and a greater number of administrators and support staff. The *Ordedienst* was instructed to spend no more than five hours on an outgoing transport, but practically, from the time the Commandant received his Jewish quota from the Hague to the moment the doors closed on the wooden freight cars, the entire process consumed about forty-eight hours. Within that span Westerbork's bureaucrats and their aids prepared and typed the transport lists; checked, hauled, and loaded the baggage; ministered to the sick, kept order, and supplied the provisions.

The quota of Jews for each transport was determined at the headquarters of the Security Police in the Hague and transmitted to Gemmeker by telex. Then a meeting took place in Gemmeker's office attended by the Chief Administrator, Kurt Schlesinger, and two of his assistants in the registration department; Dr. Spanier, the chief medical officer; one or two additional department heads; and the leader of the Applications Office, Dr. Ottenstein.

Though there always were many items on the agenda for discussion, in the last analysis the only criterion that mattered was numbers. Gemmeker would open the meeting by informing the Jewish officials of the total number of Jews requisitioned by "the Hague." Next, each department head supplied a status report of his administrative area, detailing the availability of "transport material," that is, who was and who was not expendable. Questions concerning time frames, provisioning, baggage handling, police deployment, as well as anticipated difficulties and problems, were structured into directives with which the Jewish officials would then return to their offices.

Rudolf Fried, the businesslike head of the Central Card Index, was one of the first to receive this quota, usually from Schlesinger, on Sunday afternoon or evening. Fried thereupon told his workers to start pulling the cards of all "transport-free" inmates. Each worker was responsible for one or more letters of the alphabet. After all the names had been pulled, they were sorted into two basic lists, one by alphabet and the other by barrack. The alphabetical list was for the German authorities, including the "Green Police" that accompanied the transport. The *Ordedienst* received a barrack copy, as did the barrack leaders. Of both lists there had to be eleven copies.

The list with the names of "transport-free" Jews was to be completed at least a day before the transport, but as the list continued to be revised right up to the very last moment, the deadline was rarely met. With all the last minute changes and the haggling and bargaining by department heads for the lives of their friends and acquaintances, Fried stated after the war that "the typists of my department frequently had to work until deep into the night to get the transport list ready."

At approximately three o'clock in the morning a Jewish camp official or the barrack leader—known by the inmates as the "Angel of Death"—entered the barracks with the lists of names of those selected for that morning's transport. Everyone whose name was called had to indicate his or her presence. After the Angel of Death had made his lugubrious visit, the barracks were overrun by personnel from Administrative Section Ten, Education and Welfare. These aided with the packing to ensure that no one exceeded the single allowable blanket or the baggage weight limit of fifteen kilos. The belongings of the deportees were piled in front of the barracks for collection by the Flying Column and taken to the train for loading.

The External Division of the Welfare Department saw to a "quick and smooth resolution of the transport" by assisting with the preparation and distribution of provisions, inspecting the sanitary conditions on the trains, bathing and dressing the orphans on the transport list, and outfitting the deportees with water flasks, mess-tins, mugs, rucksacks, forks, knives, and spoons. In these and scores of other chores, the Welfare staff worked closely with hundreds of people from Administrative Section Five, the Internal Service. According to the latter's year-end report, on days of large outgoing transports the functionaries of this department were wont to work anywhere from thirty-six to forty-eight hours at a stretch.

Probably the hardest working individual before a transport was the exemption officer, Dr. Ottenstein. On the day before a transport he often worked through the night in an eleventh-hour effort to obtain exemptions for inmates whose transport status was still in doubt. But even when the effort succeeded in temporarily reprieving a number of individuals, it could hardly be called a victory. The quota itself was inviolate, the numbers were unalterable, so that any such exemptions were to be replaced by others. Sometimes the Applications Officer actually managed to pull a victim from a train at the very point of departure, as in the case of the woman whose head and skull measurements later substantiated her claim of being of Aryan descent.

Not counting such peak periods as the first half of October, 1942, when thousands upon thousands of Jews left within days of one another, the deportation system worked to perfection. This model efficiency was due to the labors of transport workers stimulated less by the desire to excel than by the universal tenacity to survive. Their own fate depended on a plentiful and regular flow of "transport material." To these prisoners every inbound train bringing fresh human supplies for the East was a welcome sight. "[W]e have to be cruel," the anonymous baggage handler of the Flying Column put it bluntly, "since it comes down to this: they or we."

As they witnessed the endless exodus of Jews from Westerbork, those whom fate had temporarily spared became immune to the suffering around them. Even though their own status was merely put in abeyance, they became deaf to the cries that filled the barracks the night before a transport and actually came to resent the tumult of grief. Feelings of guilt arising from their share in the deportation proceedings tended to further solidify their callousness. They had reduced life to the single principle of survival at any price. In the beginning, before this principle had perverted their natural affections, they might show susceptibility to sympathy by the exhibition of whatever mercies were in their power. Thus, in preparation for the transports of July 15 and 16, 1942, the first ones out of Westerbork, the inmates collected money, food, and clothing for the deportees and constructed sleeping bins in the freight cars. It would remain the only act of its kind.

Initially Dr. Ottenstein used to cry at the transports, "but not later." Later, he stated after the war, all he felt after working through the night of a transport was hunger, "a very ordinary feeling of hunger." In a postwar deposition, Dr. Elie Cohen stated that he used to get all spruced up whenever he had registration duty at an incoming transport.

> We made ourselves pretty for this occasion. I shaved, put on my best suit, a clean shirt, a clean white overcoat, polished my shoes extra hard. And then you went

to see your friends who also had registration duty. The women made themselves up nicely, a touch of rouge on the cheeks, lipstick, nails exquisitely manicured. You then cheerfully had a drink beforehand.
[. . .]
At about one-thirty [a.m.] you went to the registration hall. A few were already there. Although there was no alcohol, there were soft drinks and cigarettes were sold on the sly. . . . People flirted and dates were made; the latest news would be swapped. Nothing could happen to us. Didn't all of us have [exemption] stamps! To be sure, we were Jews, but actually rather superior Jews. . . . When Schlesinger entered you began to bow and scrape. A German atmosphere prevailed: the clicking of heels and kissing up to the boss. And yet you participated and called it being flexible. You were terribly flexible in order to save your own life. And then the news came that *one* was about to arrive.

Etty thought it the worst thing about Westerbork, this flattening of human sensibilities. People no longer wanted to think or feel, only to forget—"As if suffering in whatever form it strikes us, isn't also part of being human." The trouble with forgetting was that it undermined the Jews' ability to cope with camp life; not wanting to think or feel made them blind to the plus side of their suffering, for "every new situation," Etty declared, "has the potential for enriching us with new insights." It had always been her belief that suffering ought to make people stronger, not weaker; better, not worse. But how many in Westerbork were like Mechanicus, who told her that, live or die, his recent tribulations had made him a more serious and deeper person. Etty prayed that the shared affliction of Jews and non-Jews in this war would not be for nought; that from it they might yet draw some meaning on which to build anew.

There are things, Mechanicus once told Etty, you cannot write about, only experience. One of those things, certainly, was the night before a transport. When she sat down to write her impressions of the night of August 23, 1943, Etty was fully aware that in this case words hide more than they reveal. The only metaphor she could think of to describe it was to say that she "was in hell." She was overwhelmed, mystified, and for once completely at a loss for answers. "What is going on?" she burst out. "What kinds of enigmas are these? In what kind of fatal mechanism are we enmeshed? . . . Here we are up against deeper questions. . . ."

No one who has read that letter is likely ever to forget it, and here, in Etty's own words, are some the scenes that made her think she was in hell.

> Yesterday afternoon I once again went through my sick barrack, going from bed to bed. Which beds would tomorrow be empty? The names on the transport list are not released until the very last moment, yet some already know beforehand whether or not they have to go.
>
> A young girl calls me. She is sitting bolt upright in her bed with wide open eyes. It is a girl with thin wrists and a transparent, narrow face. She is partially paralyzed. She was just beginning to learn to walk again, between two nurses. "Did you hear? I have to go." We look at each other for a while without speaking. There is nothing left of her face: she is all eyes. At last she says in a plain, drab voice: "A pity, isn't it, that everything you've learned in life counts for nothing." And: "How hard it is to die, isn't it?" All of a sudden the unnatural stiffness is shattered by tears, as she shrieks: "Oh, that I have to leave Holland, that's the worst thing of all!" And: "Oh, that I wasn't allowed to die sooner. . ." Later on in the night I see her again, for the last time.
>
> In the wash-house I encounter a smallish woman, a basket of dripping-wet laundry under her arm. She grabs hold of me. She looks rather haggard. She pours a stream of words over me: "It can't be, it's not possible that I have to go. And I won't even be able to get my wash dry before tomorrow morning. And my child is

ill, has a fever. Can't you fix it so I won't have to go? And I don't even have enough clothes for the child. I just now received some small pants instead of the large ones. It's making me go crazy. And you're only allowed to take one blanket—one blanket; nice and cold we'll be, that's for sure. I have a cousin here. He came the same time as me but he doesn't have to go because he has a fine set of papers. Do you think that might work for me, too? Please tell me I won't have to go. What do you think, will they leave the children with their mothers? Yes, come back again tonight. Will you be able to help me then? What do you think, those papers of my cousin. . ."

It is impossible to tell who has to go and who doesn't. Nearly everyone is up. The sick help dress one another. There are some who don't have a single item of clothing; their luggage has either been lost or hasn't gotten here yet. Women are moving about from the "Welfare." They are distributing clothing, regardless of whether they fit or not. It doesn't really matter, as long as you have something against your body. Some of the older women are starting to look rather ridiculous in their outfits. Bottles of milk are being prepared to send along with the infants whose wretched screeching penetrate through every seam of the barracks. A young mother says to me, almost apologetically: "My child never cries otherwise. It's as though it knows what's going to happen." She lifts the child, a delightful baby of eight months, out of its primitive crib and laughs at it: "If you're not nice you can't go on the trip with mama!" She tells me about acquaintances: "The time when the green police came to get us in Amsterdam, the children cried up a storm. Then father said: 'You'd better be good or else you won't be allowed to get in the green car and the gentleman in green won't take you with him.' And that did it, the children quieted down." She winks at me bravely, a small, dark woman with a witty, olive-colored face, dressed in gray slacks and a green woollen sweater: "I'm not so tough, even if

I'm laughing now." The woman with the wet wash is almost at her wits' end. "Can't you hide the child for me? Come on, hide it. It has a high fever, how can I take it with me?" She points at a little bundle of a child with blond curls and a red-hot little face. The child is tossing and turning in a little bed made of rough wood. The nurse wants to put an extra sweater on the mother, over her dress. She protests: "I'm not taking anything with me, what's the use . . . my child." She sobs: "A sick child they take away from you and you never get it back." A woman approaches her, an ordinary, heavy-set working woman with a kind, flat face. She pulls the desperate mother down beside her on the rim of an iron bedstead and speaks to her in a voice bordering on the musical: "You're just another ordinary Jew, aren't you; you have to go, too, right. . . ?" A few beds further down I suddenly spot the freckled, ash-gray face of a colleague. She is kneeling beside the bed of a woman who has taken poison and is dying. It's her mother. . .

"God almighty, what's going on here, what's the idea?" escapes me. She's that petite, affectionate woman from Rotterdam, a real proletarian. She is now in her ninth month. Two nurses attempt to dress her. With her misshappen body she leans against the bed of her child. Beads of sweat run down her face. She's staring into a space where I can't follow her and says in a flat, worn-out voice: "Two months ago I volunteered to go to Poland with my husband. But then they wouldn't let me go because my deliveries are always so difficult. And now I have to . . . because someone escaped tonight." The wailing of the infants swells, filling every nook and cranny of the ghostly-lit barrack. It's almost unbearable. A name comes to mind: Herod.

On a stretcher, on the way to the train, she started going into labor, and then they were allowed to take her to the hospital instead of to the freight train, which on a night such as this certainly deserves to be ranked among the great humanitarian deeds. . .

I pass by the bed of the paralyzed girl. She is already

partially dressed, thanks to the help of others. I have never seen such big eyes in such a tiny face. "I can't take it," she whispers to me. A few paces away stands the hunch-backed little Russian woman whom I've mentioned to you before. She stands there, wrapped in sadness. The lame girl is her friend. Later she complained to me: "She didn't even have a plate. I wanted to give her mine but she didn't want it, saying; "I'll be dead in ten days anyway and then these awful Germans will have my plate." She stands in front of me, a green silken kimono around her small deformed body. Her eyes are like those of a very wise, innocent child. Remaining silent, she first gives me a long, searching look: "I wish, oh how I wish, I could float away in my tears." And: "I miss my dear mother so terribly much." (This dear mother died here a few months ago in the wash-house by the toilet, from cancer. There at least she found a moment by herself in which to die.) She asks me, in her peculiar voice and in the tone of a child begging for forgiveness: "Surely, the good Lord will understand my doubt in a world such as this, won't He?" Then, in an almost loving gesture of infinite sadness, she turns away from me, and the whole night through I see a deformed, silk-green form moving among the beds, extending a tiny hand to those that are leaving. She herself doesn't have to go yet, at least not this time. . .

I am squeezing tomatoes into bottles for the babies who are leaving. Next to me sits a young woman. She looks enterprising, very well groomed, and ready to go. It almost sounds like a cry of liberation when she exclaims, tracing a wide arc in the air with her arm: "I'm going to embark on the big journey, maybe I'll find my husband." A woman across from her interrupts her bitterly: "I have to go too, but I wouldn't call it embarking."

I take a good look at the woman next to me. She has only been here a few days, having come from the punishment barrack. There is something soothing and self-assured about her. The small mouth hints at defiance. Dressed in slacks, woollen sweater and woollen vest, she has been ready for the outbound journey since nightfall. On the floor beside her lies a heavy rucksack with a rolled up blanket. She tries to stuff a few sandwiches down her throat. They are covered with mould. "I'm sure this won't be the last time I'm eating mouldy bread," she laughs. "In jail I didn't eat anything for days." A smattering of her story in her own words: "I can't tell you how they humiliated and insulted me there. I had the misfortune of telling them that I couldn't stand up and then they kept me standing for hours on end, but I never gave a peep." She looks defiant: "My husband was also imprisoned there. They really beat him, but he was tough, really tough! He was sent on last month. Just then I happened to be in my third day of labor, so I couldn't go along. But he was really tough!" She almost beams. "Perhaps I'll find my husband." She laughs defiantly: "Even if we rot and become filth, we're gonna make it through!" She looks at the crying babies around us: "I shall be very useful in the train; I still have mother's milk."

"What, you too?" I suddenly call out, appalled. Between the rumpled beds of the restless and wailing infants a tall figure of a woman approaches, hands gripping the air in search of support. She is wearing a long, black, old-fashioned dress. She has an aristocratic brow and snow-white hair, piled high on top of her head. Her husband died here a few weeks ago. Although she is long past eighty, she doesn't even look sixty. I always admired her because of the stately manner in which she lay on her shabby bed. Her answer comes in a gruff shriek: "Well, I wasn't allowed to lie next to my husband in the grave."

"Well, look who's here, too!" It is the lively little ghetto woman who always lay so hungry in bed because she never received any packages. There were seven of her children here. Terribly resolute and busy she toddles about on her short legs. "Yeah, what do you think. I have seven children and they need a tough mother to go with them, right?" She rapidly stuffs a gunny bag full of clothes. "I'm not leaving anything behind. My husband was sent on a year ago and my two oldest boys are also gone already." She beams: "My children, they are such darlings to me!" She trundles, she packs, she bustles, and has an encouraging word for every passerby. A small, ugly ghetto woman, with black, greasy hair, fat stomach and short legs. She is wearing a shabby dress with short sleeves. I can think of her wearing it standing behind her washtub in the *Jodenbreestraat*. Now she is going to Poland in the same dress, three days' travel, with seven children. "Yeah, what do you think, I'm going with seven children and they need a strong mother to go with them, right?"

Everything about that young woman over there shows that she once used to live in luxury and was very pretty. She has been in the camp only a short time. She had gone into hiding because of her baby. Now she is here through betrayal, like many others who went underground. Her husband is in the punishment block. She looks miserable. Here and there the originally black hair breaks through her dyed blond hair with a greenish gloss. She is wearing several layers of underwear and clothes on top of one another. After all, you can't carry a whole lot, especially when you're taking a small child. Now she looks deformed and ridiculous. Her face is blotchy. She looks at everyone with opaque, questioning eyes, like a young, completely defenseless animal delivered up to the slaughter. What will this woman, who already looks so completely shattered, look like after three days of travel in the overcrowded freight train in which men, women, children and babies have been squeezed along with their baggage, with a barrel in the center as the only stick of furniture? They will probably be taken to other transit camps, from which they will be shipped further on. We are being chased right across Europe.

Two weeks after writing these lines Etty herself climbed into the cattle car to Poland. Wagon No. 1 held her parents and her younger brother, Mischa. Her older brother, Jaap, was deported seprately. Etty was in wagon No. 12.

Seeing Etty off that September morning was her friend Jopie Vleeschouwer. After the train had left, Jopie returned to his barrack and wrote a letter to Etty's friends in Amsterdam. The letter described Etty's last hours in the camp.

Etty had been in good spirits, Jopie reported. She actually seemed glad finally to be going. "I have my diaries [the diaries she kept in Westerbork; they were never found], my small Bible, my Russian grammar and Tolstoy with me, and who knows what else." On the way to the train she had joked—though admittedly some of her jokes were rather tinged with melancholy—and "chatted cheerfully, a kind word for everyone she met on the way." Before getting into her own wagon, she had taken leave from her parents and Mischa in wagon No. 1, and had briefly stopped by wagon No. 14 to look for a friend who had won a last minute reprieve. As the train pulled away from the platform, Etty's hands were among those that waved, and her voice among those that sang.

Singing, however, had been the furthest thing from Etty's mind when she first received the news of her going. The tiding came late Monday evening, September 6, and caught her completely off guard, months of prior mental preparation notwithstanding. Her first reaction was one of shock, wrote Jopie, but "within the hour" she had pulled herself together and had started packing.

The order decreeing the Hillesums' deportation had come especially from the Hague and bore the signature of the Higher SS and Police Leader in the Netherlands, Rauter himself. Etty's mother, prompted by her son Mischa's unwillingness to forsake the family, had written to the Nazi chieftain requesting that Mischa's exemption be extended to the family as a whole. Rauter's answer was to cancel Mischa's exemption and to order the immediate deportation of the entire family. Heretofore Mischa, one of Holland's most promising young pianists, had been exempted as a 'cultural Jew,' guaranteeing Theresienstadt at the minimum.

Etty herself had never lifted a finger to keep from being

deported. That, she explained, was something she could only do for others, never for herself. Her own strength—"and it was a great one," she conceded—lay in acceptance and suffering, not in doing. She also considered it to be morally wrong to covet a *Sperre*, because you were only saving yourself at the expense of somebody else. She said she had seen enough of that ugly syndrome during her stint on the Jewish Council. "I don't want all these little scraps of paper for which Jews are killing each other," she had exploded the year before after a *Sperre* had inadvertently fallen into her lap.

> I would like to be in every one of the camps scattered throughout Europe, on every front. I don't ever want to be so-called "safe." I want to be there, and on every spot that I am I would like to bring all these so-called enemies a little closer together. I want to know what is happening in the world . . . and share this knowledge with as many people as I can possibly reach.

Etty wanted to see and experience everything for herself—as a Jew, as an artist, and as a chronicler, "the eyes and ears of a fragment of Jewish history." That was why, Jopie related, she was depressed about going to Auschwitz with her parents. Her father, an impractical sort, needed constant watching; she had never gotten along with her mother. Mischa had a history of mental breakdowns. Seeing them suffer, attending to their needs, would drain her of her energies, she feared, and keep her from observing and experiencing things to their fullest.

One would have to think that Etty's fears turned out to be groundless. Most probably, her father and mother were gassed immediately upon arrival, and Mischa, with his delicate mental make-up, soon thereafter.

Could Etty's going have been avoided? asked Jopie at the end of his letter "No! It apparently had to be this way," he reflected. Yet Jopie was confident she would return. "People like Etty," he said, "have a knack for pulling through the most difficult situations."

Etty is believed to have been gassed at Auschwitz on November 30, 1943.

5

Max, Willy, and Erich
CABARET

"When you're up to your neck in shit, what's there to crow about?"

From "Humor and Song"
(September 4, 1943)

The Commandant makes his appearance shortly before eight o'clock. Magisterially he strides down the aisle at the far side of the Big Barrack. As he passes, the audience rises. By the time he reaches his seat—a plush upholstered chair, front row center—the entire audience is on its feet.

Like a conductor calling his musicians to order, the Commandant thrusts his arms up into the air and keeps them there until all is quiet. When they finally come to rest again at his sides, all of the spectators are back in their seats. Pleased, Commandant Gemmeker lowers himself into his own chair. His retinue, the Aryan subordinates and his Jews-in-waiting—Todtmann, Schlesinger, and Spanier—occupy their stations on either side of him.

It is Saturday, September 4, 1943, opening night of "Humor and Song," Theater Group Westerbork's newest cabaret.

Was it only four days ago that the knife struck again, uprooting another thousand Jews—men, women, children? Only yesterday that the Commandant announced that the Hague had ordered the closure of the camp and the "resettlement" of all inmates to East?

None of it seemed to have made any difference. Ticket sales for "Humor and Song" were brisk. As always, the house is packed.

In the wings, the entertainers are poised to go on. Nervously they await their cue. They have been rehearsing for weeks, day in and day out. Just this afternoon they went through a full dress rehearsal, before a select group of invited guests. They even worked on their routines and the timing of the jokes in the morning of last Tuesday's transport, when ordinarily they would have been required to remain in their living quarters until after the train's departure. Gemmeker's orders: the show must go on. Tonight they will be playing for their lives. The Commandant is in the audience.

At eight o'clock sharp the orchestra in the pit strikes up a jolly tune. The floodlights come on. Behind the curtain, the entire cast has massed for the opening number, appropriately titled "Roll-Call! Roll-Call!" Thus the audience finds the cast, momentarily frozen in a funnel of light, when the curtain finally parts. The yellow stars on the entertainers' costumes glitter and sparkle from every part of the stage.

A lively blend of comedy, song, and dance, "Roll-Call! Roll-Call!" sets the pace and pattern of a show built primarily around the theme of life at Westerbork. Westerbork without tears. For upwards two hours, through eighteen numbers in all, the performers frolic and caper on the boards, extracting a thin residue of mirth from the encoiling tragedy. They sing of love— of the love between "A girl from the "V" [Welfare] and a boy from the O.D.,"—and of happiness, a special kind found only on the moor. At the piano Willy Rosen, an entertainer with a "little house" to his name, self-mockingly intones:

> I have a house with such comforts
> That I feel like a regular homeowner.

Others poke fun at the inmates' lack of *Arbeitsfreude*, the universal contempt for work:

> Whoever is a glutton for work
> And fails to shirk
> And works himself to the bone
> Is a drone and a jerk.

And: "Up with work! So that no one can touch it!"*

In the crowd that evening is Mechanicus. He has not come to amuse himself, but, as always, to observe and to record. Sitting quietly, he studies the reaction of the people around him. This evening, he notes, the response is not uniformly enthusiastic. Only the young folk seem to be able to let go completely; the older people admire the performers and enjoy the songs and the skits, but their response lacks vigor. A one-liner, delivered as if cued from offstage, brazenly fixes the responsibility for the unusually somber mood: "When you're up to your neck in shit, what's there to crow about?"

Seasoned veterans, the performers know what to do with a listless audience. They exhort their patrons to sing and clap along with the tunes. Soon the hall is alive with singing and

---

*Author's translation from *In Depot*.

114

clapping, presumably to such refrains as, "Yes, it's true my friend, only on the moor can I find happiness," and, "When a package arrives, There is sunshine even when it rains."

Shortly before ten, the entire cast once more gathers on stage, marking the end of "Humor and Song." The applause is warm and generous. The show has "come off." "A faultless performance put over very professionally," concedes Mechanicus.

The inmates scramble for the exits. Curfew is at ten—two hours later than usual.

Among the cast that materialized on stage for the finale was Max Ehrlich. What Kurt Schlesinger was to the administration, Pisk to the O.D., and Dr. Spanier to the hospital, Max Ehrlich was to Westerbork's entertainment life.

Ehrlich, a German Jew, was no stranger to the audience, not even to the Dutchman in it. Before settling there permanently in 1939, Holland had been a regular stop on his entertainment circuit. Between the wars, the Dutch were wild for German popular culture, and Max Ehrlich was among Germany's best in cabaret. By the time he mounted the stage at Westerbork, his face was comfortingly familiar.

The German Jews knew him even better. Particularly the Berliners among them remembered him when he was both a comic and an actor specializing in comedy parts. In a city bursting with talent Max Ehrlich ranked near the top. His Menelaus in Max Reinhardt's lavish production of Offenbach's *Die Schöne Helena (La Belle Hélène)* at Berlin's Grosses Schauspielhaus may well have been his finest hour on the stage.

But the impersonal grandeur of the Grosses Schauspielhaus hardly figured as the ideal setting for the likes of a performer whose natural turf was the Kurfürstendamm, Berlin's Champs d'Elysée. And it was on the Kurfürstendamm, with its sidewalk cafes, bright lights, and celebrated nightclubs, that Max Ehrlich made his mark. Berlin society gathered at the *Kabarett der Komiker,* a phantasmagoria of entertainment featuring Germany's biggest movie stars and entertainers. One reason they came was to see Max Ehrlich.

With Hitler's victory in 1933, Ehrlich's career as a "German" comic and actor came to an abrupt *finis*. On March 30, Germans learned from their radios that on April 1 they were to join a boycott of Jewish-owned businesses and services. Less than a week later the first laws aimed at ejecting the Jews from the national body—the so-called "non-Aryan legislation"—surfaced in the *Reichsgesetzblatt*, the official register of laws promulgated by the government. Fearing harassment, Jews were urged by their leaders not to draw attention to themselves.

Jewish entertainers must have thought that the caveat was specifically directed at them, because every performance featuring Jews invariably produced a jeering claque of Nazis. In Max Ehrlich's case—a performer whose forte lay in cabaret, a genre with a considerable Jewish presence and a reputation for iconoclasm—strict compliance with this unwritten law was not an option but an unavoidable necessity.

Hounded from the "Aryan" stage, Ehrlich took his talents elsewhere. Though he continued to call Germany home, his bags were seldom unpacked for very long. With sizable colonies of German émigrés in Zurich and Bern as well as in Holland, and the popularity of German-style cabaret at an all-time high, Ehrlich's services did not go begging.

When he continued to perform in Germany itself it was strictly before Jewish audiences as a member of the Jewish Cultural Union. The Cultural Union had been created in 1933 with the dual purpose of giving work to unemployed Jewish performers and providing diversion for a Jewish public that was unwanted at "purely German" entertainments. Writing and performing his own sketches, farces, and songs, Ehrlich soon emerged as one of its leading attractions. With titles such as "Oil and Vinegar," "Tutti Frutti," and "All Aboard, Please," the fare Ehrlich brought to the stage of the Cultural Union was similar to that which would later amuse the crowds at Westerbork.

For six years Ehrlich found a congenial home with the Cultural Union, performing in and away from Berlin. Then came the *Kristallnacht*, November 9-10, 1938, the first official Nazi pogrom. For Max Ehrlich, as for thousands of other German Jews, the night of the shivering glass and crackling flames

Large barracks. Courtesy of Rijksinstituut voor Oorlogsdocumentatie, Amsterdam.

Westerbork "street" scene. Courtesy of Rijksinstituut voor Oorlogsdocumentatie, Amsterdam.

Religious service. The inscription on the curtain reads, "The Torah is Our Life." Courtesy of Rijksinstituut voor Oorlogsdocumentatie, Amsterdam.

Tailoring workshop. Courtesy of Rijksinstituut voor Oorlogsdocumentatie, Amsterdam.

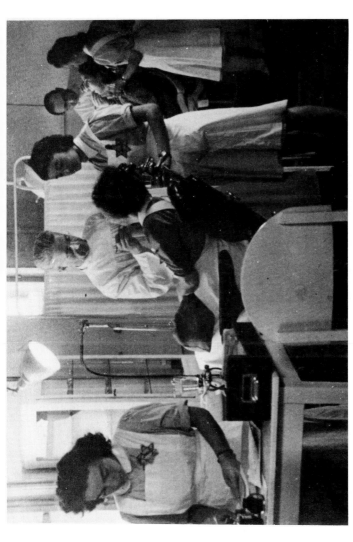

Tooth clinic. Courtesy of Rijksinstituut voor Oorlogsdocumentatie, Amsterdam.

Cabaret in the Big Barrack. From left to right: Willy Rosen, Esther Philipse, Mara Rosen, Erich Ziegler. Courtesy of Rijksinstituut voor Oorlogsdocumentatie, Amsterdam.

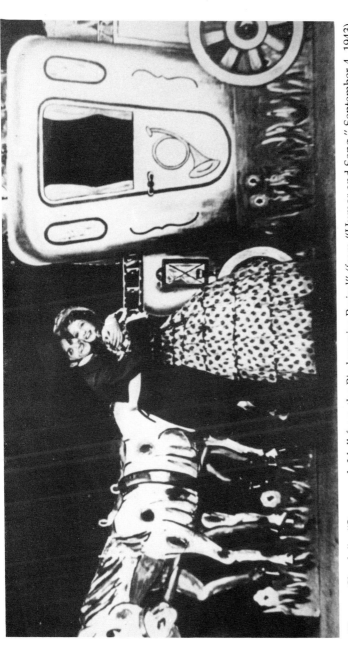

"Ever so Slowly"—"Stagecoach Idyll from the Biedermeier Period" (from "Humor and Song," September 4, 1943). Courtesy of Rijksinstituut voor Oorlogsdocumentatie, Amsterdam.

Friedrich Weinreb in 1942.
Copyright: Uitgeverij
Meulenhoff, Amsterdam.
Courtesy of
Rijksinstituut voor
Oorlogsdocumentatie,
Amsterdam.

Friedrich Weinreb in 1971.
Copyright: Algemeen
Nederlands Persbureau,
Amsterdam.
Courtesy of
Rijksinstituut voor
Oorlogsdocumentatie,
Amsterdam.

Philip Mechanicus.
Courtesy of Rijksinstituut voor
Oorlogsdocumentatie, Amsterdam.

Max Ehrlich.
Courtesy of Nederlands
Theater Instituut, Amsterdam.

Esther Hillesum.
Courtesy of J. G. Gaarlandt.

Ordedienst leader Pisk instructing Westerbork's Messenger Squad on the parade ground. Courtesy of Rijksinstituut voor Oorlogsdocumentatie, Amsterdam.

Commandant Gemmeker, Frau Hassel, and dog. Courtesy of Rijksinstituut voor Oorlogsdocumentatie, Amsterdam.

The Commandant's house (picture taken from underneath a transport train). Courtesy of Rijksinstituut voor Oorlogsdocumentatie, Amsterdam.

All set for an incoming transport. Courtesy of Rijksinstituut voor Oorlogsdocumentatie, Amsterdam.

Boulevard des Misères. Courtesy of Rijksinstituut voor Oorlogsdocumentatie, Amsterdam.

Transport. Courtesy of Rijksinstituut voor Oorlogsdocumentatie, Amsterdam.

Commandant Gemmeker at a transport to Auschwitz. Courtesy of Rijksinstituut voor Oorlogsdocumentatie, Amsterdam.

About to depart. Courtesy of Rijksinstituut voor Oorlogsdocumentatie, Amsterdam.

was the final outrage. He made up his mind to leave Germany for good.

Holland was a popular destination for Jewish entertainers fleeing from Nazism. Some merely made that country a stop-over on their way to Paris or Hollywood. Others, attracted by the kinship in language and the familiarity of the surroundings, decided to stay on permanently. Still others stayed because no other country would have them. Max Ehrlich entered Holland in 1939.

In April of that year Ehrlich had given his farewell perform-ance for the Cultural Union. By all accounts, it was a moving goodbye. At the conclusion of his performance, a one-man show entitled *Kleines Nachtlokales* (Intimate Nightclub), the spec-tators jumped to their feet and roared their approval. They shouted, *"Leb' Wohl, vergnügter Tausendsassa!"* an untranslatable Austrian idiom roughly meaning, "Take care, delightful little devil." On April 14, the *Jüdisches Nachrichtenblatt*, the only news-paper Jews were allowed to publish, paid him a final tribute. "In troubled times," wrote the Nazi-supervised organ, "you have taught us that we must not forget the ability to laugh."

The ability to make people laugh served Ehrlich well in Westerbork. For almost two years it kept him from being de-ported. But it is unlikely he would have succeeded as well as he did without the collaboration of two other showmen, Willy Rosen and Erich Ziegler.

Max, Willy, and Erich had known each other long before a common fate dumped them in Westerbork. Ehrlich and Rosen could trace their friendship and professional association as far back as the 1920s. After 1933, Rosen had occasionally collabo-rated with Ehrlich on shows for the Cultural Union. He had worked more consistently with Ziegler, however. Throughout the thirties they had toured together in Germany, Switzerland and Holland. In Holland they had divided their time between nightclubs in Amsterdam and Scheveningen, a beach resort on the Dutch coast popular with both native and German Jews.

Rosen was perhaps the most talented of the three. He was

certainly the most versatile. Ziegler shone at the piano; Ehrlich excelled at comedy. But Rosen, the complete entertainer, wrote, composed, and performed. He had a special talent for writing *Schlagers*—hits, catchy tunes. Audiences everywhere recognized him by his distinct call: *"Text und Musik . . . von Mir!"* Rosen was a bundle of energy.

At the time Germany invaded Holland the three men felt quite at home there. They had their families and their careers, which at first the Nazis did nothing to stop. Indeed, one of their biggest fans was Konrad Aus der Fünten, the head of the Central Office for Jewish Emigration. Aus der Fünten was responsible for implementing the ghettoization policy in Amsterdam, routinely the first step in the Nazi annihilation program. He did not seem to mind coming to a ghetto theater like the Hollandsche Schouwburg to see his favorite artists perform; their talents would even draw him to Westerbork. After the cessation of the cabarets in May, 1942, and the start of the transports two months later, the emigration chief used the Schouwburg as a central point for concentrating Jews prior to shipment to Westerbork.

By May, 1943, the three separate parts of Westerbork's entertainment dynamo had linked up, Rosen being the last to arrive. Amazingly, within the short span of a year and a half, the team would generate a total of six original variety shows.

It must have been shortly after Rosen's arrival that the trio, either collectively or through an emissary, raised the idea of starting a cabaret with the Commandant. Gemmeker was all for it. And why not? He would have his own theater company. The fantasy of power would be augmented, the legend of his munificence broadened. Probably he was bored and craved diversion. Cabaret would help keep people's minds off the transports. And the greatest concentration of cabaret talent in all of Europe would be at his fingertips: Ehrlich, Rosen, and Ziegler; Jetty Cantor, formerly with the *Deutsche Rundfunk*, Germany's national radio network; the incomparable comic, the proverbial fat man, Franz Engel; Jonny and Jones, the popular singing duo from Amsterdam; the dance master, Otto Aurich; the quick-witted M.C. Jozef Baar whose rhymes came faster than other people's speech; and Camilla Spira. Once the Commandant chivalrously walked Camilla "home" after a performance and gave her a parting handshake. *Gruppe Bühne Westerbork*—Theater Group Westerbork—was born, with Ehrlich at the helm.

Gemmeker was not disappointed. The first revue, presented that summer, proved so great a success that the Commandant, who saw it several times, virtually gave the *Bühne* leaders carte blanche for the next show. He allowed them to expand the cast (thus adding to the exemptions) and to spend lavishly on the sets, lighting, costumes, wigs, and related stage paraphernalia. One show is reputed to have cost as much as 25,000 guilders, a huge sum in those days. Westerbork's buyers, a select group of inmates authorized to travel throughout Holland to procure the camp's necessities, were handed shopping lists on which appeared the costliest items, including velvets and silks. Rarely did they return with their orders unfilled.

The camp's show people were also invited to help themselves generously to the supplies in the warehouse and to raid the workshops for labor and material. Alluding to the first privilege, the program notes of the final show, "Totally Nuts," presented in June, 1944, jokingly announced: "For the sets we have spared neither cost nor effort. . . . the material will be found missing from Industry the next time it takes inventory." By the same principle, days before a premiere, the workers of the carpentry and tailor shops would be kept so busy preparing the sets and costumes that all other work would be shelved until after opening night.

Combining elements of revue and cabaret—songs and sketches—the shows put on by Ehrlich and company rested on formulas that had worked in the past. Creating a show was simple, said Willy Rosen. All you needed was two comedians, one fat and one skinny; about five pounds of "sex appeal," a couple of catchy tunes; some old jokes and a lot of new ones; three or four sets; a mix of red, green, and white lights, and, presto! the revue was ready. It all had to look unrehearsed, therefore much rehearsing was in order. And no politics.

The whole was geared to the cultural level of the public. The skits revolved around dieting, fashion, the battle of the sexes. The dancing was mildly suggestive. "The Westerbork Girls Dance!" from "Bravo da Capo," shown in October, 1943, featured a chorus line of young women revealing ample leg—precisely the kind of entertainment the Nazis blasted as being decadently Jewish. "The Idiocy of Dieting" (from "Totally Nuts," June, 1944), had Lisl Frank instructing the ladies in gymnastics. The same show brought the sketch "Ten Minutes of Inventor Delirium!"—"Not for those with weak hearts!" cautioned the program notes. "Tamed Beasts," a "recipe for taming disobedient housewives" appeared in the March, 1944, revue "Variety Evening." Proceeding randomly among the six shows, other sketches and songs bore titles like "Street Music"; "I Sing for You, Jonny"; "Tonight I Counted the Stars"; "Everything Goes Better with Humor"; "Your Old Suit is Still Good, Bobby"; "I Can't Wait for You, My Man"; "You've Been Thinking of Someone Else for a Long Time"; and "Carnival! Carnival!"

Performed almost entirely in German, Westerbork's revues oozed with sentiment, schmaltz, nostalgia, and romance. "Ever so Slowly," for example, from "Humor and Song," was described in the program notes as a "Stage Coach Idyll from the Biedermeier Period," the nineteenth-century German equivalent of the Victorian age. It featured a pair of lovers wooing one another in and around a stagecoach with the driver acting as a foil to their passion. The same show brought back the 1880s in "I Fell in Love during a Waltz." The April, 1944, cabaret "Variety Evening" revived "The Good Old Operettas."

On one occasion the entertainment triumvirate tried their hands at a revue-operetta. Born in Berlin around 1930, revue-operettas were musicals consisting of a dozen or so tunes woven around a popular theme song. There was no plot to speak of and nearly all of them dripped with sentiment. Among the most popular of the genre was Robert Stolz's *Zwei Herzen in Dreivierteltakt*. A number of German émigrés in the U.S.A. successfully adapted the formula to the American film and stage.

Ehrlich, Rosen, and Ziegler brought the revue-operetta to Westerbork. Their handiwork took up the entire second half of "Totally Nuts!" "Are we ever meshugge," teased the program notes, "now we're giving you a regular opera!" Written by the "librettist in residence," Willy Rosen, with music by "Maestro" Erich Ziegler, and starring "our irresistible comic pair, Max Ehrlich and Franz Engel" and the "ever popular prima donna

Lisl Frank," Theater Group Westerbork was proud to present *Ludmilla oder Leichen am laufenden Band (Ludmilla or Corpses on the Conveyor Belt)*. Not to worry, though, the notes reassured. Willy Rosen had arranged a "happy ending."

The Commandant liked his cabaret so well that he decided to put some of it on film. His film, *Westerbork*. Fittingly, the cabaret scenes open with a shot of two-thirds of the camp's entertainment triumvirate, Willy Rosen and Erich Ziegler. They are seated in the orchestra pit, at two adjoining uprights, revue-style. Nattily attired in suits and ties, they look very pleased, very much in their element. Their fingers fly across the keyboard with the greatest of ease. On the stage itself, the camera catches Jonny and Jones in the midst of a standard vaudeville number. The two singers from Amsterdam, decked out in skimmers, candy-striped blazers and plain pants, glide back and forth across the stage in unison, arms linked, canes twirling. Jonny and Jones are followed by a couple of routines featuring Esther Philipse, a pretty blonde in her late twenties. In the first Philipse, a mainstay of the Westerbork cabaret, acts out a fantasy of becoming a new cabaret star. Starting out in a dress, a flamenco dancer's hat and a tambourine, she finishes in tight-fitting shorts swaying over a saxophone like a jazz musician. Stage-struck, she likes her new stardom so well that at last someone has to come and drag her away.

Two straight comedy acts—one featuring two men engaged in a bowtie-snapping duel, the other of a hapless gent on a bench caught in the line of fire between two squabbling, saliva-spraying women—precede the final cabaret sequence of the film. It stars Jetty Cantor, also blonde and attractive. Dressed as a man, in pants, shirt, and tie, and smiling demurely, Jetty sings and plays the violin. Just before she finishes, the rest of the cast emerges from the wings and stations itself on Jetty's right and left. The moment she stops playing, the audience bursts into wild applause. Basking in the acclaim, the entertainers beam with delight, blowing kiss after kiss at the spectators below.

Like the camp itself, the stage on which Ehrlich and company luxuriated in their momentary glory had an inauspicious beginning. It had been nailed together with timber salvaged from a gutted synagogue in Assen. That was in the fall of 1940, while Schol was Commandant, and a department known as Development and Diversion (*Ontwikkeling en Ontspanning*) began ministering to the inmates' recreational and spiritual needs.

For its inaugural production, presented in November, 1940, the inmate-organizers of Development and Diversion selected Shakespeare's *A Midsummer Night's Dream*. Apparently the most memorable thing about that production was that two ministers had come especially from the Hague to see it. Little did the spectators then suspect that the barrack, the Big Barrack, which presently resounded with their laughter ere long would not be big enough to hold their tears. Nor could the actors have known that one day German dignitaries, each attended by a not-too-Jewish looking female, would there toast the deportation of the forty thousandth Jew from Westerbork.

Apart from its production of the Shakespeare comedy, little is known of D and D's subsequent programming. The department ceased to exist altogether when the camp formally passed into German hands in July of 1942.

After the Nazi takeover, Westerbork's entertainment life did not get back on track until well after the deportations had become thoroughly routinized. The resumption and expansion of recreational activities coincided with the camp's rapid evolution into a full-fledged community with a lifebeat of its own. Along with the administration, hospital, industries, and workshops, Westerbork's entertainment life flowered prodigiously, particularly within the year spanning the summer of 1943 and 1944, despite the fact that at the outset of this period the number of Jews shipped eastward already accounted for more than half of those ultimately deported. But because of the relatively sustained influx of fresh recruits for "resettlement" and the marked abatement in the deportation schedule itself, Westerbork's impresarios would be assured that they would not have to go begging either for participants or spectators.

Hence, the Ehrlichs among the inmates had no trouble delivering a veritable smorgasbord of entertainments. For sport buffs there was boxing, track and field, and soccer. Played at the camp's inspection ground, the soccer games especially drew large, enthusiastic crowds. Whenever a Jewish team faced an all-Aryan squad, as happened on occasion, the whole camp seemed to gather at the place where human feet had worked the sand into the consistency of smooth cement. In these interracial contests it was, of course, better for Jews if they walked away losers.

Boxing matches were held in the Big Barrack. One such took place on the evening of September 25, 1943. It was attended by the Commandant and F. H. Konrad Aus der Fünten, who besides cabaret shared Gemmeker's passion for fighting. On the card that night were three bouts, each from a different weight class, bantam, welter, and middle. The punctilios of the sport were meticulously observed. Each boxer, decked out in the "Jewish colors," blue on white, entered the arena with a second at his side and a doctor in his corner. A referee inside the ring enforced the rules while three judges at ringside kept score. Evidently the Camp Sport Administration executed its mandate with the same zeal for perfection that stamped Westerbork's bureaucracy as a whole.

For cabaret and sport the Commandant had a bottomless appetite; for classical music none. Not once did he attend a performance of the Westerbork symphony. His interest in classical music was confined to a ruling banning the playing of non-Jewish composers. Of course a Nazi had no business going to "Jewish" concerts—Mahler, Bloch, Mendelssohn, Saint-Saëns. But neither did he go when the ban was temporarily lifted for the benefit of the Protestant Jews and the program featured Liszt, Schubert, and Weber.

The driving force behind the camp's musical life was the *Gruppe Musik—Lager Westerbork*. This too was a hardworking unit. Under its aegis, musical formations proliferated. It put together a chamber music ensemble, a choir, and a thirty-to-forty member symphony. The symphony was stocked with some of Holland's finest musicians. Some had even played with the Amsterdam Concertgebouw. *Gruppe Musik-Lager Westerbork* also supplied a small band for the cafe which in the fall of 1943 started doing business out of a corner of the Big Barrack. On Sunday evenings inmates could listen to popular music there while sipping ersatz drinks.

In July, 1943, Gemmeker suddenly ordered an end to all performances of classical music. The injunction came at a time when rumors charging favoritism at the tryouts for the Commandant's beloved cabaret were rife. Camp Order No. 42 decreed the cancellation of the upcoming Sunday concert and threatened to cut off classical music altogether should the rumors persist.

That was the official reason Gemmeker gave for terminating the concerts. But in private he told Dr. Ottenstein that he was stopping the concerts because classical music was too taxing for working people—the same reason the Nazis at home gave to justify inundating the airwaves with easy listening music. The Commandant simply did not care for classical music.

Commandant Gemmeker was by no means alone in preferring popular to classical music, "light" to "heavy" entertainment. The overwhelming majority of the prisoners shared with their master a marked partiality for boxing, soccer, *Schlagers*, and comedy. But of all the diversions Westerbork's entertainers brought to the moor, none pleased the inmates more than the cabarets. For weeks on end, the hit songs and jokes of the latest revue would be on everybody's lips. Performances were always sold out well in advance, and competition for tickets was so keen that Westerbork's ticket sellers were repeatedly reminded to handle the distribution in a way which would avoid friction.

Despite or because of their suffering and the patent anomaly of laughter amid sorrow, the inmates continued to flock to the cabarets. And the reason they kept on going, not once but many times over, was that they felt compelled "to live with the living." This was the "law of life," concluded Mechanicus, which Gemmeker, in allowing "the Jews to amuse themselves," appeared to have invoked at Westerbork. But whether or not he was doing so consciously was a question the diarist left in abeyance. In fact, the "law of life" cited by Mechanicus—a law which rules man and by which man can be ruled—was the most powerful weapon in the Nazi war against the Jews. So effective was this law that the prisoners of the death camps would "deny" the final reality even as their lungs breathed the ashes of destruction and their eyes beheld the instruments of doom.

Likewise at Westerbork, where week after week train after

train rumbled eastward, the inmates told themselves that they went to the cabaret mainly out of curiosity, so that after the war, as Mechanicus put it, they "would be glad to chat about everything that went on at Westerbork." But what their attendance really added up to, he knew, was that they did not want to miss their evening out. In other words, they simply went in order to escape, to forget for a few hours the burden of existence. And for many the price alone was incentive enough. Being of the poorest sort, these jumped at the chance to see something for a paltry ten cents.

But at bottom it was not price but release that mattered, wrote Dr. Ottenstein after the war, to "forget for a few hours all cares and dangers." And to resist its pressure was as futile as fighting off sleep after a long period of wakefulness. The Application Officer recalled what happened to a "serious man" who tried. After resisting for months, he simply gave up and of an evening treated himself and his family to the Lethe of the cabaret.

Westerbork's cabaret bred the illusion that things were not as hopeless as they seemed. The splendor of the settings, the elaborate costumes, the glitter and make-believe world of the stage—all of it was opium to already blunted and often thoroughly depleted sensibilities.

But there were some who never lost sight of the real Westerbork. For these, a small minority, there was no erasing the shocking contrast between a barrack which by day served as a registration center for incoming prisoners, soon to be deported, and by night was transformed into an amusement hall. "Barbed Wire," a poem by one R. Pool, pointed up the hideous disparity:

> Typewriters, crowds of people:
> Children waiting in the throng;
> Names and date and place of birth
> Last address, occupation and I.D.'s;
> Pushing and shoving—get a move on;
> Typewriters banging away;
> Camp pass and barrack number;
> Noise and stench and fear and sorrow;

Typewriters in a gloomy hall;
They enter the camp—avalanches of suffering.

—Stagehands—one hour to go;
Floodlights; the stage is set—
The same hall (quickly, slaves, on the double!)
The curtain rises on the show:
>   "Best of all I like the moor, only on
>   The moor can I find happiness!"
>   [. . .]
Applause: a man at the piano:
>   "The words and music are by me—
>   I have a little house, so pretty and pleasant;
>   I have a chair, a table and a toilet."
>   We sleep in barracks as in a barn
>   In bunks three-high, thick as a wall.
>   We sit on long benches
>   And eat amid the stench of lysol
>   And wash ourselves in a crowd.
>   We are never alone—a nightmare
>   And go about with sorrowful faces
>   To the latrines in long rows.

"I have a house with such comforts
That I feel like a regular homeowner."

The entertainers who found favor with the Commandant were an envied lot. They had exemptions, "little houses," and the promise of Theresienstadt. They were admired. Work in their field gave them a sense of personal worth and identity not vouchsafed other prisoners. Used to playing roles, they adapted more readily to camp life and bore up better under the strain. On stage, before a captive audience, they seemed to be able to forget the what and the wherefore of their internment.

But when the lights dimmed, the curtain fell, and the costumes were put away, illusion was laid to rest and with it the performer. He was returned to real life. He lined up for roll call, sorted foil, peeled potatoes, cleaned toilets, hauled luggage, typed forms. Etty Hillesum found the performer odious and pitiful who by day wheeled the belongings of the deportees to the transport train and at night basked in the adulation of the cabaret crowd. She spoke of him with biting irony and unvarnished contempt.

> Among them [men from the Flying Column] I discover two of the commandant's court jesters, a comedian and a song-writer. At one time one of them was scheduled to go on transport. But a few evenings earlier he literally sang as if his life depended on it before an excited audience, which included the commandant and his entourage. He sang, "I can't understand why the roses are in bloom," and more such current hits. The commandant, who knows rather a lot about culture, thought it beautiful. He got his exemption. He even got a little house, where he now lives behind red-checked curtains with his peroxide-blonde wife. She sweats out her days behind a wringer in the steaming-hot washhouse; and there he goes, straining over a wheelbarrow containing the baggage of his fellow Jews. He looks like a walking corpse. And, over there, goes another court jester, the commandant's favorite pianist. Of him it is said that he plays so brilliantly that he can even play Beethoven's Ninth as a jazz number, and that's not something to sneer at. . . .

In broad daylight Westerbork's cabaret folk were indistinguishable from their neighbors. Like them, they exhausted every means to stay off the trains. Unlike them, they nearly succeeded, leaving the camp on some of the very last. For much as the Commandant might have liked to save his court jesters, he could not. *Kriegssituation.*

And so, on September 2, 1944, the roles were reversed. This time Commandant Gemmeker mounted the stage and the entertainers were in the crowd below. The entire camp population— several thousand—had been summoned to the Big Barrack for an important announcement. Orders had come from the Hague, Gemmeker announced, to "evacuate" the camp. Three hundred inmates would stay at Westerbork for maintenance.

During the next few days two trains left Westerbork, one for Auschwitz, the other for Theresienstadt. Ehrlich, Rosen, and Ziegler were put on the latter. At the *Musterlager* Ehrlich and

Rosen were put on another train—to Auschwitz. Only Ziegler survived.

Showman till the end, Willy Rosen spent his last moments at Westerbork writing an ode to the camp. The librettist of the comic opera *Ludmilla or Corpses on the Conveyor Belt* called it "Goodbye of a Long-Term Resident." The ode nostalgically evoked the happy hours he had spent at the transit camp on the heath, its many hardships notwithstanding.

Goodbye of a Long-term Resident

My dear Westerbork, I now must take my leave,
On account of which I sadly grieve,
Though you often treated me harsh and unkind
Yet you remain peaceful on my mind.
My Westerbork, you vexed me a great deal,
And yet you had your own kind of sex-appeal.
Now I softly say, "Goodbye" dear boiler-room;
A final whistle and all is gloom.

Goodbye my bookshelf, goodbye my pantry,
You gave me much joy, you came in handy.
Goodbye my beloved stew and garbage pail,
I am packed and sacked, ready to hit the trail.

Many a transport I saw leave from here,
And now—now I myself bring up the rear.
Now I am getting on the train, rucksack and all,
Just between you and me: it's no ball.
But save your advice and your compassion,
I'll be just fine; I am going in soldierly fashion.
Just give me, give me my extra chow,
I leave with butter and much know-how.
I packed everything; I am leaving nothing behind,
I'm even taking my wife, my greatest find.

Now I am sitting in the train; the whistle blows,
And for the last time my glance over Westerbork roves
And now I'm going; I'm filled with suffering
Goodbye my Westerbork, P.O.B. Hooghalen.

6

Friedrich

SPERRE

I was a dealer in soapbubbles. I gave the people who came to me a soapbubble with which they could dream a little longer before they were taken away.

Friedrich Weinreb, interview with journalist Henk de Mari (June 1973)

Who is Weinreb? Weinreb is a swine rebbe,
Weinreb is the friend of the gentlemen in the Hague;
Who is Weinreb? Weinreb is a swine rebbe,
Weinreb sends the Jews from Portugal to Prague.

Inmate song

During the winter and spring of 1947 a number of powerful international Jewish organizations rallied to the defense of a Dutch Jew accused of collaboration. "Our informants are convinced of Weinreb's innocence," wrote the World Jewish Congress in a letter to the Dutch ambassador in Washington. The same organization cabled the Dutch Minister of Justice in the Hague. Friedrich Weinreb, it asserted, "at the risk of his life saved hundreds of Jews from deportation and certain death." Pleading Weinreb's case, the world body of Orthodox Jewry even approached the Dutch Queen Wilhelmina. "I appeal to your majesty," wired the president of the Agudat Israel from New York, "in behalf of Frederick (sic) Weinreb long time social worker in good standing now held custody for twenty-two months on basis of unproved accusations. Many witnesses testify his courageous work during occupation saving number of persecuted already doomed people from certain death."

These organizations were not the biggest champions of Friedrich Weinreb's innocence, however. The biggest champion was Friedrich Weinreb himself. From his jail cell the alleged collaborator kept a busy schedule lambasting those he said had put him there. There were rather a lot of them. According to Weinreb, their number comprised all those to whom the concept of heroism was utterly foreign: civil servants, bureaucrats, burghers, conformists, cowards, ingrates, hypocrites, and collaborators. People like that, Weinreb said, were only capable of dragging everyone down to their own level.

In April 1947, with his trial about to come up, an English language version of the lamentations of Friedrich Weinreb, in his own hand, was being readied for the American press. The author saw it as the starting point of a global drive to bring about the restoration of his honor. An advance copy reached his lawyer later that month. "I myself feel," Weinreb explained in the attached cover letter, "that this case goes far beyond my immediate person. It is a mean, hypocritical affair . . . it gives me a wonderful feeling to have told the truth . . . for truth I'll gladly do time."

Weinreb's brief to the American public was six thousand words long. It claimed that during the war he had risked his own life to save "hundreds of Jews." The opening two paragraphs represented the statement of the case:

A Dutch Jewish economist who started and operated single handed an underground organisation for
the protection and safeguarding of his fellow-compa-
triots, thereby saving the lives of hundreds of Jews, is
still kept in jail by the Dutch authorities NOW:—two
years after the complete liberation of the Netherlands
by the Allies. This unbelievable fact throws a gloomy
light on the utterly abnormal conditions, under which
operated the "Directorate of Special and Political Juris-
diction" in Holland.

In the early and darkest period of the War—in
1942—the Gestapo gave the Dutch police-force (not a
Nazi organisation) order to round up the Jews by ten
thousands to be deported to the extermination camps
in Poland. At that time there existed not yet a well
organized underground movement which could properly deal with the situation and take care of unfortunate men, women and children. One single Jew, Fre-
deric Weinreb, since many years member of the
Netherlands Economic Institute (financed by the
Rockefeller Foundation) decided to take action, without anybody's help, and evolved a plan so fantastic in
scope and design, as will only be equalled by few other
mystery plots in recent underground-history.

Weinreb's "American" essay never made it to print. About
to go on trial, he was advised to cease all propaganda activities.
The fervent appeals of his transatlantic friends also went un-
heeded, and the case came up as scheduled. On Tuesday, May
27, at 10:00 a.m. sharp, the accused was led before the Special
Court dealing with "political delinquents" meeting for the first
time in public session. Thus began a trial which to this day has
kept Holland divided between those who glorify Friedrich
Weinreb as the shining star of the resistance and those who see
him as a Judas.

The prisoner who entered the packed courtroom in the
Hague that spring morning hardly seemed the type to have
masterminded what the prosecuting attorney in his opening
statement execrated as the "greatest swindle ever perpetrated in

the Netherlands." Before the bench came someone with the looks and demeanor of a scholar, a rabbi possibly; at any rate, completely inoffensive.

But there was nothing inoffensive about the crimes of which Weinreb stood accused. The Special Court heard testimony from witnesses who accused the former economist of having swindled large sums of money out of Jews marked for deportation to Westerbork and the death camps by pretending he had a "list," approved by the German High Command, which would enable those on it to emigrate to South America in exchange for foreign funds and German prisoners. Prosecution witnesses related how Weinreb had betrayed the trust of scores of inmates in Westerbork who had looked upon him as their savior. The court also heard testimony that he spied on former cellmates with whom he had shared a brief imprisonment in a Nazi jail for such privileges as kosher food, proper lighting for his religious readings, and other considerations for the unimpeded practice of his faith. There were allegations that Weinreb had betrayed hundreds of underground Jews by helping the SS locate their hiding places; that he had sold Jews for a dollar a head; and that he had traveled freely and without a star throughout Nazi-occupied Europe as an agent of the SS in the company of other SS officials.

Weinreb took the stand and denied it all. He insisted he could answer for everything he was accused of having done between 1942 and 1944, and that he alone was capable of defining the "morality" of his actions, even though these involved the lives of others. "I indeed defrauded the people," he told the court, "but I did it with good intention." He admitted he had tricked Jews into believing his emigration list—actually there were several—was real. But he had also urged them to take other steps to save themselves. The net result, he claimed, had been positive. The money from the emigration scheme was spent finding people places to hide and supporting them thereafter, and by "paying off" the Nazis he had saved more Jewish lives. It could not be proven, he said, that he had spied on Jews and turned them over to the Nazis; he had never consciously betrayed anyone.

It was all very confusing. Only the prosecuting attorney seemed to be absolutely sure of his man. "His story," inveighed

Mr. P. S. de Gruyter, "is one piece of self-glorification; the accused never stops talking about the enormous sacrifices he and his family made to save Jewish compatriots and of the notorious game he played, twice over, with the notorious *Sicherheitsdienst*. But never were things so beautiful and marvelous as the accused depicts them. As I see it, everything was done with only one thing in mind: the preservation of his family."

The trial went through a number of sessions before reaching judgment at the end of November. Weinreb was sentenced to three-and-a-half years imprisonment, with credit for time already served. The sentence was not a popular one. Mr. de Gruyter especially was unhappy and immediately filed an appeal with a higher court. The prosecuting attorney wanted ten years—the same punishment Commandant Konrad Gemmeker would receive for sending 80,000 Jews to the gas chambers.

Though it convicted Weinreb primarily for treason and spying, in its judgment the Special Court actually downplayed the element of treason. Treason being difficult to prove, it chose instead to emphasize the broad consequences of his lists, as would the Special Appeals Court which in October, 1948, revised the sentence upward to six years. These courts concluded that Weinreb's "emigration list," by fostering false hopes, had stopped the participants from considering other means of saving themselves. Both courts also ruled that Weinreb had used his lists to save himself and his family, to pay off the Nazis, and to make a bundle in the process. But only the appeals court held that their overall impact, calculated as a ratio of life over death, lay on the negative side.

Despite increasing his sentence to six years, due mainly to several additional proven cases of spying, the higher court held with the lower that Weinreb's original intentions had been good. But "the legal order," the appeals court lectured, "does not condone that a single individual, trusting in his own powers and moral standards, disposes in such a manner of the lives and fates of others." In so holding, in conceding nothing to the special conditions that obtain in time of war and occupation, the court, said Weinreb's defenders, had made criminals out of all resistance fighters, not just Weinreb.

A substantial part of the press seemed to agree that something was amiss. The Special Court's investigation into Weinreb's wartime activities, though it had taken a year and a half, was criticized as having been incompetent and as having failed to establish Weinreb's guilt beyond a reasonable doubt in the trial itself. The general consensus was, as one journalist put it, "There is something fishy here." Others complained about the dyed-in-the-wool antisemites and former officials of the *Sicherheitsdienst* called to the stand as government witnesses. There were rumors that some of these ex-Nazis had been mistreated by government investigators in order to get them to testify against Weinreb. A respected Catholic weekly spoke of a "Wild West in the Hague" and blasted the government's handling of the case as so shoddy it "would make for a black page in some two-bit Balkan police state."

As it turned out, Weinreb did not serve out the entire six years. He was released in December 1948, after a successful appeal by his lawyer for a year's remission of his sentence on the grounds of illness in the family (Weinreb's wife was suffering from lingering mental disorders) and the automatic reduction in the sentences of all political prisoners with good prison records that accompanied the accession to the throne of Queen Juliana. When asked to sign the release papers, he refused. It was the sabbath. The authorities did not insist.

Today Friedrich Weinreb lives in Zurich, Switzerland, wears a Talmudic beard, studies, and says his prayers. A small, spry man in his mid-seventies, he lives by the principles and rituals of his faith. During the thirty-five years that have passed since his trial, he has immersed himself in biblical exegesis, the Cabala, Jewish philosophy, law, and morality. His cerebrations of ancient Hebrew wisdom have taken him to places like Indonesia, Turkey, Germany, and Israel. His followers have sought him out in Switzerland, his permanent home since 1968, to attend his lectures on the scriptures and for refresher courses in Judaism. And there too, in *Die Gesellschaft für die Sinnverständnis der Bibel*, he has gathered about him a small group of devoted disciples who hold their teacher, their rebbe, in holy awe.

The bookshelves in Weinreb's modest Zurich apartment attest to the range of his erudition. They contain hundreds of books in many languages. The works that have flowed from his own pen have a niche to themselves. Strange hermeneutics, steeped in the mysticism of numbers, they crackle with random observations on the here and now, which he flays with a gusto reminiscent of the Old Testament prophets. Science and technology, he says, are to blame for the current blight on man's soul, for his pessimism, his despair, and immorality. And the Jews? "I am," Weinreb has been quoted as saying, "the last remaining Jew."

With his long white beard and Orthodox ways, Weinreb does in fact resemble something vestigial. He evokes the memory of Jewish Orthodoxy as it existed at one time in eastern Europe. The evocation is not altogether inappropriate. He was born in 1910 in Lemberg, today's Lvov, then a city of 300,000 on the eastern fringe of the Austro-Hungarian Empire.

The Weinrebs left Lemberg in 1914, fleeing war and pogrom. Two years later they entered Holland, settling in Scheveningen, a resort town on the Dutch coast. Scheveningen was home to a sizable colony of Eastern European Jews, refugees like themselves. Hard years followed. They barely made ends meet. Their accents and mannerisms brought ridicule and scorn. Native-born Jews looked down on them as an inferior Jewish specie. Although they became Dutch citizens in 1927, the act of taking out citizenship had little meaning in itself—perhaps no more than a change of address. In everything else they remained Jews from Eastern Europe.

The stoutest continuator of that tradition turned out to be Friedrich, the youngest Weinreb. With time the roots that tied him to the east kept spreading and gathering strength. One of these roots led to a town not far from his native Lemberg called Tolstoye (Polish Tluste), reputedly the birthplace of the Baal Shem Tov. The Baal Shem Tov, or Master of the Good Name, was the founder of the eighteenth-century Jewish revival movement known as Hasidism. A charismatic preacher, the Master of the Good Name taught that redemption could be earned without asceticism and that every human act, no matter how simple, was sacred if done "for the sake of heaven." With this message he electrified the impoverished Jewish masses of the east. The Baal Shem Tov has also been credited with delivering the Cabala, an important source of Hasidism, from being the bloodless creed to which previous centuries had reduced it by purging it of its suffocating dogmas. Weinreb became both a Cabalist and a Hasid.

The passion for metaphysics and the mystical Weinreb claims to have had since childhood. If so, it was not evident in his choice of career. He settled on a most wordly pursuit, economics. For the doctorate he never completed he was planning to do a dissertation on the construction industry in the Netherlands, and he once won a prize for an essay on the First Russian Five-Year Plan, an achievement which initially brought him to the attention of the Netherlands Economic Institute. In the late thirties he was also a part owner of an economic consulting agency. He never experienced any conflict, Weinreb said, reconciling the sacred and the profane; he felt at home in both, but the spiritual came first.

His detractors beg to differ. All they see is a fraud. They think of him as a man possessed by greed, a man without a conscience, a charlatan and a rogue. They think even less of his work, the books on the sacred and the occult. But the book they hate the most is the one that made him rich—his wartime memoirs, *Collaboration and Resistance.*

Collaboration and Resistance—three volumes of 1,800 pages— was Weinreb's answer to his enemies. It was an instant bestseller. Though his detractors reviled the memoirs as a pack of lies, Weinreb said he was pleased. He had finally unburdened himself. He had told his side of the story. What he had done during the war, he said, was to furnish the desperate Jews of Holland with hope, a "soapbubble filled with hope." They were passive, frightened, and confused, and he lied to them so they would sleep a little easier:

> "I see a burning building, with the enemy carrying off all those who escape by the main entrance. I call out to the people in the building that the main entrance is elsewhere, and I lead them to a secret cellar. They think they are going to the main entrance and they are grateful to me. Meanwhile I save them from the enemy.

Yes, I lie and deceive them, but only to help them . . . If I had told them I was taking them to the cellar no one would have followed me.

A year and a half after the German invasion Weinreb was no longer with the Netherlands Economic Institute. A casualty of the Nazi Aryanization program, he joined thousands of other Jews similarly dismissed. Faced with a "Jewish unemployment problem," the Nazis decided to ship many of the jobless to labor camps in Drente. Each eligible Jew was told to register for the work camps with the Jewish Council and threatened with severe punishments if he did not do so. Remembering Mauthausen, Jews had learned to take such threats seriously.

From the work camps it was only a short step, figuratively and literally, to Camp Westerbork. In January, 1942, the first Jewish contingents reported to the labor camps in Drente. On May 2 the Jewish star was introduced, and after June 30 Jews were no longer allowed to leave their homes between the hours of eight in the evening and six in the morning. Thus trapped, they became easy marks for the *Razzias* the Nazis were wont to stage whenever too few of them heeded the summons of their leaders to present themselves at the train stations for shipment to Westerbork, which in July superseded the work camps as the principal center for the concentration of Jews.

It stands to reason that Jews resisted every effort to draft them into the camps, be it for labor or deportation. The offices of the Jewish Council were flooded with their petitions requesting exemptions. They suddenly contracted crippling diseases requiring hospitalization. They fled, or tried to flee, to Belgium. They claimed to be foreigners—Costa Ricans, Ecuadoreans, Salvadoreans, Portuguese, Swiss, and so forth. All were testing the walls of the Nazi *huis-clos*, probing for soft spots and cracks.

Jews with access to foreign currency thought they had found such a crack through emigration. These Jews, whose money Germany coveted to pay for war materials purchased abroad, were exempted from labor service. Their money was to be kept in a bank in neutral Switzerland until the emigrant arrived at his destination, whereupon it would be transferred to the Reich treasury. In the meantime, pending the completion of the transaction, the prospective emigrant was placed on a special list exempting him from deportation.

Probably the most popular of all such lists—and there were many though none made good on its promise—was one administered by E.A.P. Puttkammer, an executive at a large Dutch bank. Himself German, Puttkammer gradually emerged as a middleman between qualifying Jews and the appropriate financial authorities in Germany. Another such list, though less popular, was started by one J. J. Weisman, a former bank robber. Unlike Puttkammer, whose services were free, Weissman charged a thousand guilders a head. With this money he was able to live like a king. For the Jews on his "list" it was an expensive trip to Auschwitz.

Weinreb's emigration list got started in the late spring of 1942. It was then he told people that he was authorized to organize the emigration of thirty Jewish families—thirty-one, including his own. These families, he declared, would be permitted to leave Holland. They would travel by train to the unoccupied part of France, and from there another train would take them to Switzerland, Spain, or Portugal. Rich Jews in South America, he said, had underwritten the project by raising the necessary foreign currency.

Skeptics who wondered why the Germans had put a Jew in charge of so important a project were shown a letter from *Generalleutnant* Herbert Joachim von Schumann thanking Weinreb for his help in bringing about Holland's "frictionless integration" into the German war economy and granting his request to be allowed to emigrate along with thirty families of his own choosing. *Generalleutnant* von Schumann, "a rather large man, with glasses, a real German type," was an "administrative general" at the OKW, the Supreme Command of the German Armed Forces, Weinreb explained.

But there was no General von Schumann. Weinreb had made him up. He himself had written the letter. A local printshop had supplied the OKW letterhead. The names Herbert and Joachim were chosen for their ring. Weinreb thought that strung together they sounded strong, masculine.

Word of Weinreb's good fortune spread rapidly. Jews

fought one another for a place on the list. They came not only from Scheveningen and the Hague, Weinreb's immediate environs, but also from Amsterdam and points beyond. So great was the crush that Weinreb had to take on assistants to help process the flow. He also appointed people to look after the registration in the provinces as well as in Westerbork.

Soon Weinreb's emigration list held not just thirty families or "thirty groups of families" but thousands of individuals, each paying one hundred guilders—"administrative costs," he explained. Soon there was not one list but three lists, not to mention a spate of "reserve lists." And soon there were forms to fill out, passport photos to submit, and physicals to take.

In the summer of 1942 confidence in Weinreb's emigration project stood so high that a number of Jewish Council members started reserving seats on the train, even though their responsibility for the "maintenance of Jewish life" outside the camps presumably exempted them from deportation. Weinreb himself, now a man to be reckoned with in the Jewish community, was invited to join the Jewish Council in the Hague—thus keeping the von Schumann protégé out of Westerbork.

For regardless of a place on any list, all Jews sooner or later found themselves in Westerbork, and it was in Westerbork in fact that Weinreb's bogus list scored its greatest success. That summer and fall the German authorities treated Weinreb's emigration list as real, exempting hundreds of Jews from deportation. This was strange because his *Sperre* packed none of the clout of a "true" *Sperre;* its recipients had no exemption number, and their identity cards lacked the enchanted phrase, "the bearer of this permit is exempted from labor service until further notice." Apparently, the on-hand supply of "transport-free material" was so plentiful that there was no need to look for more by microscopically examining each and every *Sperre.*

However, the *Sperre* commotion in their own backyard did not escape the watchful eye of the Nazi functionaries of the Jewish Department in Scheveningen, Weinreb's hometown. In September he was picked up for questioning. His interrogator was IVB4 detective *SS Hauptsturmführer* Fritz E. Koch, described by Weinreb as a typical German *Übermensch*—tall, blond, and blue-eyed; a "decent automaton" but not very bright. Within days Weinreb had him convinced that there really was a *General-*

leutnant Herbert Joachim von Schumann, even though no one at OKW headquarters had ever heard of a general by that name. That the general was none other than the quiet, unassuming Orthodox Jew sitting across from him never seemed to have crossed Koch's mind. He thought it was a conspiracy into which Weinreb had been innocently drawn. He believed that von Schumann, obviously not his real name, intended to plant trained informants among Weinreb's emigrants for the purpose of briefing Germany's enemies on her military secrets.

In his memoirs Weinreb recounts how he tantalized the *Kriminalpolizist* with mouthwatering details about the emigration project, how it got started, and the nature of his own involvement. Koch learned that Weinreb had saved von Schumann's life by pulling him out of the path of an onrushing truck while they were both waiting for a streetcar. In requital the grateful general was allowing him and others to emigrate. Koch also learned that von Schumann walked with a cane and had at least two accomplices: an umbrella-toting German called von Rath and a déclassé squire named Six, a Dutchman.

Koch believed every word. He instructed Weinreb to carry on with the emigration project as if nothing had happened. When the conspirators made their next contact, Koch said he would nab them. On that, he released his prisoner, with orders to report to him regularly.

Weinreb's "emigrants" were amazed. A Jew had slipped through the Nazi mesh! Their confidence in his emigration list skyrocketed. It became well-nigh absolute after Weinreb, exploiting the SS connection, instituted a travel committee to regulate the technical aspects of the itinerary, appointed wagon leaders, and told the candidates what and what not to bring. He also asserted that the trains would be leaving around the end of 1942 and the beginning of 1943.

Koch could not be put off as easily. Stringing Koch along required greater ingenuity. It required nothing less than a "golem," a human automaton that does exactly what it is told. Centuries ago, in Prague, a golem fashioned from clay had rained destruction on the enemies of the Jews. That golem had been brought to life with cabalistic formulas; Weinreb's carried a price tag of 10,000 guilders.

Hendrik Gerard Kotte, a petty criminal who preferred risking jail in Holland to taking a chance on being sent to a German labor camp, was unflatteringly described by his master as a "slow-moving, utterly brutish . . . yellowish hunk of meat." This hulking mass Weinreb pounded into something resembling a déclassé squire, complete with pochette and perfume. This was the golem he played into Koch's hands as Six towards the end of 1942.

But Kotte was no Weinreb and quickly broke down, telling all. Koch was beside himself. He packed Kotte off to Dachau, where he died; he interned Weinreb's wife and children at Westerbork, and threw Weinreb back in jail. In his memoirs Weinreb recalled how afterwards Koch grabbed and shook him by the lapels, shouting, *"Jetzt ist das Theater aber aus!"*—"Now the comedy is finished!"

In telling the tale of the made-up list, the made-up general, the made-up Six—the made-up everything—he felt, Weinreb later wrote in *Collaboration and Resistance*, like the storyteller of *A 1001 Nights*. Almost daily he was hauled before Koch. Finally, in May of 1943, he was dispatched to Westerbork, stamped *S*.

With Poland looming before him, Weinreb seemed to have come to the end of his rope. Yet a month and a half after internment, he was back in his old cell in the basement of IVB4 headquarters, and three months later he was again at liberty. In yet another month he was traveling throughout Holland, to Antwerp and Brussels, minus his star. Finally, in November his family was released from Westerbork and allowed to live in the Hague.

What had happened?

What happened, Weinreb says in his memoirs, is that he hoodwinked the SS a second time.

The reason, Weinreb asserts, he was brought back to Scheveningen was that Koch wanted him to devise a scheme through which the SS might capture thousands of Jews still at large, that is, in hiding, along with their money and valuables. Refusal, Koch reputedly gave him to understand, would see him back at Westerbork and on the next train to Poland along with his family. Weinreb says he accepted Koch's offer because he was sure he could again lead him by the nose and thus save more Jewish lives.

By September he had come up with something that met with the approval of the *Hauptsturmführer*. It was his old emigration project, reconstituted to serve the current object of rooting underground Jews from their precarious sanctuaries. The updated version was practically identical to the emigration scheme that had fooled Koch so badly the year before. It also had a general, a list, a train, induction fees, and a southern destination—not France as before, but Portugal, the former having come under German occupation. In Portugal a thousand Jews would be exchanged for a thousand Germans presently in South American jails. To reduce the fear of being caught prior to setting out for Portugal, he would advise his candidates to remain in hiding until the actual day of departure. On the appointed day, gathered a thousand strong on the platform, they would be met by a contingent of SS-men who would strip them of their money and jewels and put them on a train to Auschwitz.

The large scale *Razzias* of May, June, and September 1943, coupled with the deportations of close to forty-three thousand Jews between March and November of that year (primarily to Sobibor) had cleared Holland of nearly all "legal," that is to say, full, Jews. Apart from the Jews in hiding, the only sizable group of full Jews still present in Holland were Jews married to non-Jews, and these, feeling quite secure in their exempted status, were not about to take a chance on Portugal.

With Holland mostly *Judenrein*, the only logical place for the improbable duo to operate was Westerbork. They reasoned that among its thousands of inmates, there must be hundreds with knowledge of the whereabouts of friends and relatives in hiding. By stressing the fact that the exchange was open to *all* Jews, thus implying amnesty and deliverance for the "lawbreakers," and relying on the inmates themselves to spread the word, they were hoping—or at least Koch was, says Weinreb—to lure to Westerbork some of the thousands of Jews the Nazis believed still to be at large.

Weinreb returned to Westerbork—by car, Koch driving—on Tuesday morning, November 22. News of his return and the object of his visit, Philip Mechanicus recorded in his diary, created a sensation. "I was hailed as a king," Weinreb later boasted, recalling the adulation of the inmates who not long ago had beheld in him a fellow Jew marked out for death.

After conferring—and dining, kosher no less, Weinreb says—with Gemmeker and securing his approval, Weinreb went to work. He called a general meeting, attended by an overflow crowd, and explained his new emigration project. Appointing a representative to look after the registration, Weinreb left Westerbork on November 24. Unchaperoned, he boarded a train for the Hague, traveling with his family first class and without stars.

At Westerbork the scramble for a seat on the mythical train to Portugal resembled nothing so much as a stampede. "Weinreb," wrote Mechanicus, "is the favorite."

> Applications for his list are streaming in. The majority want to go to Portugal, or, if need be, to Morocco or Brazil, as long as they can escape from the unbearable pressure, from the uncertainty of the transports. The more level-headed ask themselves: 'What is Weinreb's role in all of this? What is his list worth?' They are suspicious that he, as a Jew, has been given the responsibility by the German authorities to drum up 10,000 Jews in Europe as exchange material for Germans in South America and that he travels around Western Europe without a star . . . to carry out his program. Can that be kosher?

When the dust finally settled, as many as 1,500 inmates had a brand new *Sperre*, Mechanicus among them. Weinreb's *Sperre* lasted two months. It was revoked on February 3, 1944, "freeing" the bulk of his exemptees for the transport that left Westerbork for Auschwitz on February 8.

As for Weinreb, he was nowhere to be found. With the ax about to fall, Weinreb went underground and took his family with him. He was not seen or heard of again until after the war.

The day Weinreb's *Sperre* "smashed" in Westerbork, Mechanicus, mulling over the list's sudden demise, gave voice to a question that was on everybody's mind: "Was it a game being

144

played by the Hague," he asked, "and did Weinreb have a part in it?"

It was not until almost a quarter of a century after the postwar courts answered Mechanicus' musings with a six-year jail term for the former "emigration expert" that the question was being asked again. With Euromart prosperity and a well-behaved German neighbor, the Dutch had found it easy to forget. Meanwhile, Friedrich Weinreb was not doing so well. In 1952 he spent several days in jail for embezzlement, and in 1957 he was twice fined for practicing medicine without a license. His difficulties with governments were not confined solely to Holland. In 1956 he was forced to resign a teaching post at the University of Jakarta, Indonesia, after running afoul of the university administration, and four years later he was expelled from a lectureship in Turkey, allegedly for falsifying examination results. Back in Holland, in 1968, a Dutch court sentenced him to eight months in prison for impersonating a physician to "commit immoral acts on women." The same charge had figured in his 1947 trial when he was similarly accused of having acted as a "gynecologist" to inspect the female candidates for "emigration." Fleeing the country, Weinreb never served the 1968 sentence. A year later he was living in Switzerland and the first volume of *Collaboration and Resistance (Collaboratie en verzet)* arrived at the Dutch bookstores.

Collaboration and Resistance exploded on a complacent, prosperous Holland like a bombshell. Its publication tore the tissue from two decades of previously healed scars. It revived cadavers from the mass graves to disturb the thoughts of the living.

It also reopened the long-dormant question of Weinreb's war guilt. Shortly after his volumes came out a small but vocal group of sympathizers began to clamor for his rehabilitation by the Dutch government. This led to the creation of a special committee by Holland's State Institute for War Documentation which proceeded to reinvestigate the charges against him with a zeal seldom encountered in government agencies. It was almost as if Weinreb himself had taken up residence at *Herengracht* 474, so completely did his spirit pervade the Institute's Amsterdam headquarters for the duration of the inquiry. For years the investigators gathered and gleaned, sifted and sorted, checked and double-checked, wrote and rewrote. At last, after nearly six years of hearings involving hundreds of witnesses as far apart as Tel Aviv and Los Angeles, the committee issued its final report. And again Weinreb was found guilty, this time even more overwhelmingly than during his first postwar trial. In their conclusions the committee members reinforced all the old charges, found a few new ones, and summarized that Weinreb was "one of the most successful fantasts of the Second World War" whose every action was governed by "personal desires for power, money and sex."

Ironically, then, the investigation by the Netherlands State Institute for War Documentation which had been ordered by the Dutch Minister of Justice on the chance that there might have been a miscarriage of justice in the 1947 and 1948 trials actually turned out less favorably for Weinreb than the findings of the earlier courts. These, at least, had not doubted his original good intentions. Less charitable, the compilers of the two massive, folio-sized volumes of *Het Weinreb Rapport (The Weinreb Report)* indicted the wartime exploits of the best-selling author in their entirety and flayed him mercilessly for invoking a "higher truth" and a "pseudo-religious" motivation to justify his deeds. As an only positive character trait they left him his undisputed talent for consoling the desperate.

Yet, strangely enough, the Institute concluded that the net effect of both emigration lists had actually been positive—not to the tune of the 525 years of life Weinreb calculated to have salvaged from the carnage—but positive nonetheless. The state's investigation was able to ascertain "with some degree of certainty" that the first list had saved the lives of twenty-one persons and had postponed death for scores of others. And although the second list had lowered the chances of survival of around sixty participants, with the loss, possibly of twelve lives, it had also increased the life-span of twelve others. Finally, it was conceded that being on Weinreb's list materially improved one's chances of survival, from the 20 percent that was the Dutch-Jewish rate as a whole to a range of 28 to 38 percent.

From the start of the committee's investigation many Dutchmen felt that dredging the muck of wartime guilt was a mistake. From Switzerland, Weinreb himself had spoken against the voices seeking to restore his honor. There was nothing further to be gained. He could see that from certain standpoints he "might not have been unjustly sentenced" during his war crime trial. Neither would he give a flat denial of the "gynecology" conviction of 1968. He also admitted that he might have exaggerated a little in his memoirs. But what really mattered, he insisted, was what he said in *Collaboration and Resistance* regarding Holland's *Entjuding,* the speedy phenomenon by which the country's Jews vanished by trainloads at a time into the extermination mills of the East. He reveals it as a story of betrayal on a mass scale.

What were the Dutch doing while 100,000 Jews were leached from their midst? Very little, writes Weinreb. The milkman continued to make his deliveries, the policeman wrote out tickets, and the mail arrived on time. Meanwhile, thousands of Dutchmen joined the Nazi hunt for Jews, collecting so many, in fact, that the Gestapo had difficulty in handling the numbers. Solid burghers robbed and even murdered Jews, turning them in for their bicycles. The queen and the cabinet had fled to England, and Holland's administrative centers and police departments bowed agreeably to the directives of the New Order. "Everyone played the game," Weinreb accuses, "even the government."

Collaboration and Resistance dismisses the fond postwar notion of a heroic Dutch resistance to the Nazis as "ridiculous," a "fairy tale"—hence the memoirs' subtitle: *An Attempt At Demystification.* Resistance, says Weinreb, barely surfaced until near the end of the war when German defeat was assured. At his trial in Jerusalem, Eichmann reported that the task of making Holland *Judenrein* was never a problem. Things went smoothly there, Weinreb adds, because of the collaboration of large numbers of Dutchmen and the apathy of the masses. And it is against this background of popular indifference and collaboration that he seeks one key to the destruction of Dutch Jewry; the other being the wartime role of the Dutch Jews themselves, specifically that of their leaders who "did their duty," he says, "just as the Wehrmacht did in annihilating millions."

Weinreb's own "rescue" mission involved much scuttling back and forth between the offices of the Nazi *Sicherheitsdienst* and the Jewish Council. He was struck by the similarities; the same shoe fitted the victim, victimizer, and executioner. They were all involved in a gigantic task requiring superhuman effort. Observing the Jewish Council members at work, Weinreb found it difficult to distinguish these pillars of Jewish life from the Nazi officials with whom he dealt as an "emigration expert" on the other side. The scene was the same; a cheerful, brisk, and businesslike atmosphere—the members of the Jewish Council "would be seated on one side of the desk and the scared men and women marked for deportation would be seated on the other, and the latter would be told that they really *had* to go, that *nothing* would help." The only difference—and it was a crucial one—Weinreb noted between the Nazis and the Dutch collaborators on the one hand, and Jewish Council leaders on the other, was that the former did their job voluntarily, the latter under duress. Otherwise there was the same absorption in the job at hand, the same observance to form and macabre logic. The head of the Jewish Council in Amsterdam referred to himself as an "uncrowned king" who disparaged Weinreb's "emigration list" with its few hundred names as comprising only a minor constituency compared to his own. The rationale of the Nazi master and his Jewish captive fed off a similar taint: his duty would be done, one of Amsterdam's two Jewish Council chiefs considered, if he could save "20,000 of the best Jews," by which he meant Jews drawn from the Council's own class and social standing.

Amidst the Jewish Council members Weinreb says he was regarded as an interloper working outside the Nazi-sanctioned Jewish bureaucracy. His suggestions, he claims, of "illegality," of sabotaging German orders, were rejected with horror, an offense against respectability. "We are a proud people," one prominent member of the Jewish Council allegedly told him. "We do not cheat. History will honor us."

Weinreb noted the same blindness to reality, the same bureaucratic madness and callous discharge of duties at the other center of the Jewish administration in Westerbork. The Jewish leaders there moved heaven and earth—and other Jews—to save themselves and their families and friends. In *Collaboration and Resistance* he describes a party for these Jewish chiefs which he witnessed during one of his own brief internments there. It was held in a "salon" groaning with liquor, cigars, cigarettes, pastries, fruits and condiments, candies, and sandwiches. Jewish servants bowed deeply when presenting the drinks and canapes to their Jewish superiors. There was much laughter, much joviality, with no mention of the barbed wire and German guns outside, the trains that left regularly with their cargo of human fuel for the raging ovens. Weinreb found it hard to believe that these were Jews.

Holland never had its "Day of the Ax," the bloody postwar reckoning with suspected collaborators and war criminals that took place in most Nazi-occupied countries. Instead, the accused were brought to trial in orderly fashion and justice was administered swiftly, usually with surprising leniency. There was a strong desire to get on with business as if nothing had happened. A seal of silence seemed to have shut the book on some of Holland's darkest pages—until Weinreb's *Collaboration and Resistance* brought the country its belated Day of the Ax. For this the author never expected to be honored in his own land or by his own people. Holland's main Jewish newspaper echoed the general outcry against him, and in 1971 the City of Amsterdam hastily withdrew a literary prize it had bestowed on the work in 1970. All of Weinreb's rebuttals, in the newspapers and on television, only succeeded in inflaming the issue further, to the point where Weinreb threw up his hands in disgust and said that he was "above everything."

The Weinreb controversy in Holland quickly escalated into a contest between those who wished to leave the past concealed and the few who wanted to tear the wrap away. The point of friction was not what the memoirs related but the author's own credibility. Weinreb claimed he was being judged by criteria— his war crime imprisonment, the "gynecology" conviction, his troubles with different governments—which had nothing to do with the account set forth in his memoirs. He also complained of being made a scapegoat to expiate the guilt of others, Jews and non-Jews, for the destruction of Dutch Jewry. He was the "last of the Mohicans," Weinreb told the interviewers from the Institute, still paying for his past, his own and that of others.

But the problem was not so much Weinreb's credibility as it

was the unsettling burden of his accusations. Despite their bewildering complexity, his memoirs present a crazy quilt of threads and stitches that has been seen before, the desertion of Jews by their non-Jewish compatriots and the often unsavory conduct of their own leaders in carrying out the routines of human disposal. In Weinreb's own case, the real reason for Dutch inveighings against him has been dispersed in a cloud of hot air. There has been much talk of morality, integrity, and ethics. But irrespective of Weinreb's personal guilt in this squalid tale of cowardice and treachery, of individual and organized murder, his eyewitness account cannot be dismissed out of hand, for it tallies only too well with other such accounts, both in Holland and abroad.

Conclusion

*Inspection tour by the camp Commandant of the
camp at night. Closing shot: full moon night.
The camp with its large chimney silhouetted
against the evening sky.*

From the film script *Westerbork*

On Saturday and Sunday, April 7 and 8, 1945, there were busy doings at Westerbork. The Germans were packing. In the distance guns rumbled. The Canadians were closing in. The Germans were packing to leave.

Thanks to a radio they had managed to conceal, the remaining inmates were well informed of the Allies' progress. But although the prospect of imminent delivery filled them with joy, an undercurrent of apprehension was stirring to keep their excitement in check. With Germany's defeat just around the corner there was no telling what the final act might bring. And, as though to remind them of their continuing vulnerability, a hauntingly familiar sight greeted their comings and goings: at the platform, in mute corroboration of their fears, stood a train.

Not since the previous September had a train stopped at the siding to take on "passengers."

But they need not have worried, this jittery remnant. As all of their energies was being poured into the business at hand, the Germans had none to spare the Jews. This time the train was for the hunter, not the hunted.

And so Westerbork's 909 Jews watched the enemy pack. They saw lorries and carts piled high with furniture roll down the Boulevard des Misères, stop at the platform and being loaded onto the train. They saw cows and pigs wobble past the barracks and being shoved aboard. They saw Frau Hassel imperially directing her underlings in the loading of the one freight car she had commandeered for her personal use. Into that car vanished clothes by the armful and box after box containing the shirts and pajamas on which two Jewish seamstresses had worked for days. They saw their captors walk into the Central Kitchen, run their eyes along the provisions, and carry off whatever they fancied they needed; from their own hoard came coffees, teas, wines, liquor, and assorted foodstuffs—two freight cars full.

On Sunday evening the doors finally clanged shut, and the train started pulling out. The last train from Westerbork.

Two days later, preparing to flee himself, Commandant Gemmeker began taking the final steps towards ending the German presence at Westerbork and his own removal from office. Distressed as he must have been, he showed little emotion. If there was any consolation to be had, the *Obersturmführer* no doubt found it in the mettle of his own conduct. He had stood his ground; no one could accuse him of having broken under pressure. His handling of the ramified—and painful— disengagement process had been entirely worthy of the public persona he liked to project: cool, methodical, efficient.

Confidently he had signed his orders, as if they were his first and not his last. Shortly after the stoppage of the transports in the fall of 1944, he had calmly disposed of his administrative *chef d'oeuvre*, the Central Card Index, in accordance with the wishes of his superiors in the *Sicherheitsdienst*. A few days ago he had seen to the dismantling of the camp administration. The Swastikas had been lowered, rolled up, and put away for safekeeping. The time had come to write the final order.

> The Commandant announces: the camp is part of the front. The camp residents are under the protection of the International Red Cross. Since they are in an "exchange-internment camp," they are requested to take off their stars. Those who attempt to leave the camp do so at their own risk. In their own interest, the camp residents are requested to maintain calm and order and to keep as much as possible to their living quarters.

That same day, April 11, or the next, the Commandant met with Kurt Schlesinger to discuss the remaining details of the German exodus and the abrogation of his commandature. Westerbork, he told his famulus, had been rebaptized. It was no longer a *Durchgangslager* but an *Austausch-Internierungslager.* And would he please sign and post the announcement he had prepared to that effect. He then told the Chief Administrator that he was leaving and putting him, Kurt Schlesinger, in charge. With that, in a symbolic and comradely gesture marking the transition of power, he handed the Chief Administrator his private pistol.

On April 12, at three o'clock in the afternoon, Commandant Albert Konrad Gemmeker and Frau Hassel, his faithful mistress, sped off in a private car in the direction of Hooghalen.

Immediately thereafter Kurt Schlesinger, backpedaling

apace, turned over his newly acquired mandate to one of the few remaining Dutch officials in the camp, a Mr. van As.

Approximately one hour after Gemmeker's departure Mr. van As got up on the stage in the Big Barrack to address the inmates. But no sooner had he begun than a voice shouted from the back of the hall, "You're wanted on the telephone, sir!" "Who is it?" shouted back Mr. van As. "And the answer," Anne de Vries reported in the "Liberation of Camp Westerbork," a series of articles which ran in the *Nieuwe Drentsche Courant* from May 17 through May 25, 1945, "has an effect like a direct hit from a hand grenade."

> Suddenly everyone is on their feet, screaming, laughing, cheering, crying and moaning. All of those 800 people storm the exit, pushing and shoving their way outside, race through the camp and through the gate up the road which runs along the barbed wire fence to the camp farm. Young men and women up front, hair streaming in the wind; behind them, the others, portly, panting gentlemen, old women—everybody is running in the wild exodus . . . towards the liberators, shouting and screaming with joy.
>
> [. . .] Zielke [former head of External Service] rides back to the camp on top of the first tank. And soon Captain Morris, perched atop the tank, takes out his camera to record this unique event, the liberation of this ubiquitously notorious camp for Jews, for all time.
>
> The tanks are practically being stormed by the Jews. Girls are being hoisted on top so that in no time at all the tanks are no longer visible.
>
> Cheering, they ride back to the main gate of the camp. There the Canadians are dragged from the tanks, hugged and kissed and carried around the camp on shoulders. Suddenly a flag appears, the national tricolor, as well as an orange flag made out of parachute silk and carefully hidden from the Germans until this moment. They are taken to the flagpoles where only a few days ago the swastika flew and raised as the Wilhelmus is being sung.

One hour later the first German prisoners of war pass by the camp, shuffling, ill-clad, shifty-eyed creatures who glance stealthily at the exuberant camp population.

In the evening there is a party in the Big Barrack. . . . There are Canadian cigarettes and English cakes. German wine also appears. Signatures are being collected, also souvenirs. The Jewish girls go around with the insignia from the caps of the Canadian soldiers; all the Canadians have donned the Jewish star. There is singing and dancing, smoke billows from the open doors and the sounds of joyful voices echo across the dark moor.

The elation was shortlived. Not long after the liberation of all of Holland on May 5, 1945, the homecoming of the Westerbork Jews was marred by a horrible discovery. What had been rumored toward the end of the war now stood confirmed as fact. The relatives, friends, and neighbors with whom they had hoped to be reunited had been killed in the East. Soon the International Red Cross began compiling lists of concentration camp survivors and displaying them at various locations in Holland. For months on end the former Westerborkers, joined by returnees from other camps and the roughly 17,000 Jews who had spent the war abroad or in hiding, went out to check these lists for survivors, to ascertain who had and who had not "come back," as it was always put. Invariably they walked away from these places heartbroken and overcome with grief, as no more than 5,500 of the approximately 105,000 Jews the Nazis had dispatched to annihilation camps had actually "come back."

On the morning of December 4, 1978, I was walking on a road in the northeastern part of Holland. The bus driver who had let me off some time earlier at nearby Hooghalen had informed me that there was *geen bus naar Westerbork*—no bus to Westerbork. There was nothing for it but to walk to the site which more than forty years ago had been the first stage in the destruction of Dutch Jewry in the German extermination camps to the East, and where I first began life.

The weather was warm for the time of year. I paused to take off my jacket and to stuff my scarf into the attaché case I was carrying. Now and then a car whizzed by, too fast for hitchhiking.

As I approached Westerbork the reality of its infamous existence pressed itself on my mind. Up until the winter of 1942, when a spur was built to connect Westerbork with the main line, the first Jewish contingents had entered the camp by this same road I was walking. With a slight fillip of the imagination, I could see the thousands who had trodden the five kilometers which lay between Westerbork and the nearest railroad station—ragged processions of men, women, and children dragging such possessions as the authorities let them bring. But whether on foot or by train, it hardly mattered how they entered Westerbork, for the end result rarely varied: deportation to the East and almost certain death.

Presently the road started on a curve that gave onto the parking lot of a picnic and campground which had taken the Solar System as its theme. A sign there pointed in the direction of Westerbork. From a map of the area I learned that my course would take me through the stars and planets and past a large clearing hosting a dozen radio telescopes. After voyaging this earthbound armillary, I came upon a paved road, and ten minutes later I was standing in front of an upright red and white barrier, the gate to Westerbork. Off to its left stood a mock-up of the camp, a dovecote-like structure encased in glass showing the camp as it had been in August, 1944. Aided by a contemporary sketch, I easily located the hospital where I was born; also Barrack 50, according to the official camp "birth certificate," my first home.

I walked away from the mock-up into the former campground itself, proceeding along the same road that cut the camp in half during the war, Boulevard des Misères. Surveying my present surroundings, I found it hard to believe that today's pleasant greensward framed in the lingering light of a late autumn afternoon had anything in common with the windblown, sand-swept barren heath of the camp years. The tracks that used to run next to the Boulevard des Misères had disappeared, together with the roughly one hundred barracks that had been mounted on the campsite's granular surface. In vain did I try to form a mental picture of the camp in its original state. All that came to me was a confusion of images, a scattering of recollections gleaned from books, pictures, and talks with survivors, albeit heightened in tone from being altogether connected with my innermost being and existence. I distinctly remember thinking of Anne Frank leaving Westerbork in a cattle car and wondering whether here, in Westerbork, or later in Bergen-Belsen, where she found death, she had been able to sustain her faith in the basic decency of mankind which she expressed in the diary she kept while in hiding.

I kept on walking, knowing that at the far end of the present site some sort of memorial had been erected to the more than 100,000 Jews who had been interned here prior to being slaughtered in the East. But as I drew nearer, I saw that I had been wrong about the railroad: a section of it had been preserved as a symbolic reminder of Westerbork's place in the Nazi New Order. There was no consolation at all in the thought of its having suffered the same fate as the victims it used to carry; in seeing the rails severed about forty yards out from the terminal block and twisted skyward in a defiant curve. The memorial itself consisted of two flat gravestones, one on each side of the terminal block, bearing identical inscriptions, in Dutch and in Hebrew respectively. The inscription was from the lamentations of Jeremiah 4:18 and read:

> Men dogged our steps
> so that we could not walk in our streets;
> our end drew near; our days were numbered;
> for our end had come.

I read and reread the inscription, taking its lament out of the specific context of the recent catastrophe and applying it to the entire span of Jewish history. But the memorial itself—more accurately, the memorial in its overall setting—left me quite unmoved. What puzzled me was that the Dutch appeared to have spent so little effort on the commemoration of their country's Jewish victims of the European slaughter, considering that from this camp had proceeded the destruction of nearly eighty-five percent of Holland's Jews. Why, for example, had not even a single barrack been left standing? Oddly, Westerbork today, with its lush green turf, sprinkling of trees, and Boulevard des Misères reduced to parklike proportions, seemed far more attuned to the recreational spirit of its surroundings than to anything connected with its former history as internment camp. A nice place to walk or to have a picnic.

It was getting late, and I saw no reason for staying any longer. Before heading back, I stopped to take a few pictures of the memorial and the truncated railroad—just for the record, as I doubted that I would ever be back.*

---

*Today the former camp site is as I left it in 1979. I have learned, however, that a few kilometers up the road a more elaborate memorial to the victims of Westerbork has been in existence since April of 1983. The new memorial is housed in a low-slung, barrack-like structure dubbed Commemoration Center Camp Westerbork. The Center consists of an exhibition divided into three "Panels." The first two duplicate a permanent exhibition established by the Dutch government in 1980 in Auschwitz depicting the history of Dutch Jewry and their persecution during the Second World War. The third panel deals with Westerbork proper. It is the hope of the organizers, sponsors, and supporters of the memorial that the Center will serve the purpose of "providing information and documentation regarding the historical and actual meaning of the camp." That aim is also being furthered by another offshoot of current effort to give Camp Westerbork its historical due, the traveling exhibition known as Records of Westerbork.

Bibliographical Note

The spadework for *Boulevard* was done in the fall of 1978 at the Netherlands State Institute for War Documentation (Rijksinstituut voor Oorlogsdocumentatie) in Amsterdam. The Institute's Westerbork material falls into two broad categories, contemporary and postwar. Among the former are the documents that are listed below in section I, which also includes books that originated in the camp years, 1939–1945; Mechanicus' diary, for example. Not cited in this section are the numerous miscellaneous items that inform the text. The reports, for instance, of the camp's twelve administrative units; Camp Orders; charts, graphs, and statistics monitoring work output and fluctuations in the camp population; the film script; cabaret programs, songs, and poems; and letters addressed to the Commandature inquiring about the inmates. These, too, may be found at the Institute. Also not mentioned are the impressions gathered over the years in talks and conversations with survivors, my parents foremost among them.

The second section contains testimony furnished by former inmates in the postwar—usually, immediate postwar—period. Much of this testimony—reports, statements, declarations, depositions—is no more than a few pages long, and often bears neither title nor date. This section also contains books and memoirs written by ex-internees reflecting on their experiences at Westerbork (and other camps) published after the war.

Throughout, an asterisk marks the documents from the War Documentation Institute.

Section III lists background materials.

Unless indicated otherwise, all translations in the text are by the author.

I. Contemporary

Anon. "Uit her dagboek van een FK-man" (1 October 1942–7 October 1942).*

As, A. van. "Dagboek," (4 September 1942–4 September 1944).*

Braaf, S. J. "Uit het dagboek van S. J. Braaf."*

Hillesum, Esther. *Het verstoorde leven. Dagboek van Etty Hillesum, 1941–1943*. Bussum: 1983 (12th Edition). (*An Interrupted Life. The Diaries of Etty Hillesum, 1941–1943*. Translated by Arno Pomerans, N.Y.: 1983)

———. *Het denkende hart van de barak. Brieven van Esther Hillesum.* Haarlem: 1982 (4th Edition).

———. "Twee Brieven uit Westerbork." Bulkboek, nr. 73, Patty and Theo Knippenberg, eds, n.d.

Mechanicus, Philip. *In Depot. Dagboek uit Westerbork.* Amsterdam: 1978.

———. *Year of Fear. A Jewish Prisoner Waits for Auschwitz.* (Edited translation of *In Depot*.) Translated from the Dutch by Irene S. Gibbons. New York: 1968.

"Een stad in wording op de Drentsche Heide. Kamp Westerbork nadert zijn voltooiing." *De Telegraaf,* 14 October 1939.*

Wohl, H. O. E. "Commentaar uit Nederland." (20 August 1943; received by Bureau Inlichtingen 4 March 1944).*

II. Postwar

Anon. "Wat aan Westerbork voorafging," n.d.*

Anon. "De Ondergang van het Nederlandse Jodendom," n.d.*

Anon. "Westerbork." Ontvangen via FOD (Falsificatie Opsporingsdienst), n.d.*

Anon. "Aanwas en afname van de Kampbevolking gedurende het tijdperk 15 juli 1941 tot 12 april 1945," n.d.*

Anon. "Het Werk van de Contact-Afdeling te Westerbork," 1945.*

Alst, F. van. "Rapport inzake Contact Afdeling Westerbork." (Rapport van Falsificatie Opsporingsdienst), 1945.*

Andriesse, Henri Napoleon. "Herinneringen aan de Jaren 1942–1945," 1947.*

———. [Declaration], 1947.*

————. *Aan een zijden Draad. Herinneringen van een gedeporteerde.* Amsterdam: 1978.

As, A. van. "Kamp Westerbork. Waaraan dankt dit kamp zijn onstaan?" n.d.*

Berg, Jacques op den. [Declaration], 1947.*

Bergh, S. van den. *Deportaties.* Bussum: 1945.

————. *Kroonprins van Mandelstein.* Antwerpen: n.d.

Birnbaum, H. [Report], 1946.*

Block, Werner. "Westerbork und der Ordnungsdienst," 1946.*

Bonn, Hans. [Declaration], 1947.*

Cohen, E. A. [Declaration], 1948.*

————. *Human Behavior in the Concentration Camp.* Translated from the Dutch by M. H. Braaksma. New York: 1953.

————. *De Afgrond. Een Egodocument.* Paris/Amsterdam/Brussels: 1971.

————. *De Negentien treinen naar Sobibor.* Amsterdam: 1979.

Cohen, Hans. [Declaration], 1946.*

Cohen, J. "De antithese Nederlandsche en niet Nederlandsche Joden tijdens de bezetting," n.d.*

Corper-Blik, Roosje, [Declaration], 1947.*

Dam, Moses van. [Declaration], 1947.*

De Vries, Anne. "De Bevrijding van het Kamp Westerbork." *Nieuwe Drentsche Courant.* 17 May 1945–24 May 1945.*

Elbach-Trixer, Hans. [Declaration], 1947.*

Freudenberg, L. [Report], 1951.*

Gabel, Adi. "Kamp Westerbork in Schlagzeilen," n.d.*

Gemmeker, Albert Konrad. "Procureur-Fiscaal tegen Albert Konrad Gemmeker." [Trial, Bijzonder Gerechtshof, 3e Kamer, 9 December 1949].*

————. Proces-verbaal [Inquest] Nr. 425., Dossier Nr. 09 (April 1948).*

Haan, M. "Gegevens Betreffende het Kamp te Westerbork van Medio 1940 Tot Eind 1942," n.d.*

Hamburger-Bolle, J. [Report), n.d.*

Hollaender, A. "Das Karthotekwesen im Kamp Westerbork," 1946.*

Honey, Joseph. [Declaration], 1947.*

Israel, Kurt. [Declaration], 1947.*

Jacobson, K. [Report], 1946.*

Jong, Isidore de. [Declaration], 1948.*

Kruskal, Herbert. "Westerbork-Bergen-Belsen," n.d.*

Leefsma, Ralf. [Declaration], 1947.*

Lewenhoff-Kotowski, Karla. [Declaration], 1947.*

Loeb, W. [Declaration], 1946.*

Marx, E. "So war Es. Ein Bericht über Westerbork und Bergen-Belsen," n.d.*

Oss-West, Hilda. [Declaration], n.d.*

Ottenstein, H. "Lager Westerbork," 1946.*

Pimentel, H. [Declaration], n.d.*

Polak, Louis Ph. "Westerbork," 1955.*

Polak, Willem. [Declaration], 1947.*

Schlesinger, K. "Gesensätze zwischen deutschsprachlichen und holländischen Juden," n.d.*

———. "Persönlichen Bericht über die Organisation des Lagers Westerbork und die Gesichtspunkte, aus denen sie entstanden ist," n.d.*

Spier, Jo. *Dat Alles Heeft Mijn Oog Gezien. Herinneringen aan het Concentratiekamp Theresienstadt.* Amsterdam/Brussel: 1978.

Stein-Isser, Ruth. [Declaration], 1947.*

Wachsmann, E. A. [Report), 1946.*

Walter, Justin. [Declaration], 1946.*

Wassenberg, Berthold. [Declaration], 1946.*

Waterman, Louis. [Declaration], 1947.*

Weinreb, Friedrich. *Collaboratie en verzet. Een poging tot ontmythologisering.* Three Vols. Amsterdam: 1969.

Weisz, Josef. [Report], 1945.*

West, Isaac. [Declaration], 1948.

Ziegler, E. "Bericht ueber die 'Gruppe Buehne' im Lager Westerbork," 1946.*

III. Background

Arendt, Hannah. *Eichmann in Jerusalem. A Report on the Banality of Evil.* New York: 1970 (10th printing).

Cornellisen, Igor. " 'Jetzt können Sie mir sagen: wo ist der Schumann.' " *Vrij Nederland,* 5 May 1965.

Dittrich, Kathink; Blom, Paul; and Bool, Flip (eds.). *Berlijn-Amsterdam. Wisselwerkingen.* Amsterdam: 1982.

Freeden, Herbert. *Juedisches Theater in Nazideutschland*. Tübingen: 1964.

Gilthay Veth, D. and van der Leeuw, A. J. *Het Weinreb Rapport*. Two Vols. 's-Gravenhage: 1976.

Herzberg, Abel. *Kroniek der Jodenvervolging 1940–1945*. Third edition. Amsterdam: 1978.

Hilberg, Raul. *The Destruction of the European Jews*. Chicago: 1961.

Houwaart, Dick. *Weinreb. Een Witboek*. Amsterdam: 1975.

———. *Westerbork. Het Begon in 1933*. Den Haag: 1983.

Jong, L. de. *Het Koninkrijk der Nederlanden in de Tweede Wereld Oorlog 1939–1945*. 10 Vols. 's-Gravenhage: 1976.

Jong, Salomon de. *Joodse Oorlogsherinneringen (1940–1945)*. Franeker: 1975.

Knoop, Hans. *De Joodsche Raad. Het drama van Abraham Asscher en David Cohen*. Amsterdam/Brussel: 1983.

"Een Kreatie van het geheugen—Mulisch Ontmoet Weinreb." *Vrij Nederland*, 6 March 1971.

Nuis, Aad. "Het Weinreb Rapport." *Vrij Nederland*, 1 December 1979.

Presser, J. *The Destruction of the Dutch Jews*. Translated from the Dutch by Arnold Pomerans. New York: 1969.

Reitlinger, Gerhard. *The Final Solution: The Attempt to Exterminate the Jews of Europe, 1939–1945*. South Brunswick, N.J.: 1968.

Sijes, B. A. "Enkele Opmerkingen over de Positie van de Joden tijdens de Tweede Wereldoorlog in Bezet Nederland." In: *Studies over Jodenvervolging*. Assen: 1974.

Wielek, H. *De Oorlog die Hitler won*. Amsterdam: 1947.

Index

film of Westerbork, 30–31; and inmates, 28–29; appearance and manner of, 23, 24–25; attitude of Jews toward, 20–23; before Westerbork, 16–18; sentence of, 32; trial of, 13–16, 30–32

General Administrative Services, 43–44

German Jews, 4, 5, 6, 9, 29, 35, 37, 38, 41, 42, 48, 50, 51, 53, 62, 63, 67, 68, 69–70

Green Police, 48, 49, 99

Gruppe Bühne Westerbork. See Theater Group Westerbork

Gruppe Musik-Lager Westerbork, 123

Harster, W., 16–17

Hashera, 65

Hassel, Elisabeth, 25–26, 31, 153, 154

Health Service, 45

Hillesum, Esther, 22–23, 26, 30, 59, 67, 70, 96, 102–3, 126; and diary, 90; and Germans, 90–92; and Jewish Council, 88, 89; and Julius Spier, 89–90; and Westerbork, 87, 88, 89, 92; before Westerbork, 87; deportation of, 109–10; *Het denkende hart van de barak,* 90; *Het verstoorde leven (An Interrupted Life),* 90; letter of August 1943, 92–95, 103–8

Hillesum, Mischa, 109

Himmler, Heinrich, 23

Hollander, Han, 69

Hooghalen, 43, 97, 156

Housing Office, 44, 98

Inmates: and cabaret, 124–26; and escape, 81; and Jewish Council, 7; and Poland, 65–67; and rumors, 79–80; attitude toward Gemmeker of, 20–23; in camp administration, 40–41; reaction to Westerbork of, 70–72; registration of, 98

Internal Service, 46

Jewish Council, 6, 7, 41, 42, 43, 68, 92, 96, 97, 110, 138, 140

Jewish Cultural Union, 116, 117

Jewish Refugee Committee, 38

Jonny and Jones, 118, 121

Katyn, 66

Koch, Fritz E., 140–41, 142, 143

Kotte, Hendrik Gerard, 141–42

Lagerkommandatur. See Camp High Command

Lippmann Rosenthal, 98

Long-Term Residents, 5, 7, 35, 41, 42, 43, 62, 64, 79

Mauthausen, 9

Mechanicus, Philip, 22, 23, 27, 35, 48, 49, 60, 64, 69, 71, 72, 74, 81, 83, 94, 102, 114, 115, 124–25, 143, 144; and diary, 57–58; and exemptions, 58–61; and German Jews, 69–70; and Poland, 65–67; arrival in Westerbork of, 57; impact of camp life on, 74; in camp hospital, 57; *In Depot (Year of Fear: A Jewish Prisoner Waits for Auschwitz),* 58

Metal Sector, 45

Netherlands State Institute for War Documentation, 145; *Het Weinreb Rapport,* 146

Notbereitschaft. See Emergency Squad

Ordedienst, 41, 42, 46, 47, 48, 49, 78, 98, 99

Ottenstein, Otto, 60, 61, 65, 67, 95, 100, 101, 124, 125

Palestine Certificate, 65

Philipse, Esther, 121

Pisk, Arthur, 47–49, 50

Poland, 3, 9, 10, 18, 21, 27, 29, 64, 65, 66, 79, 80, 96

Police Transit Camp Westerbork, 5

Pool, R., 125–26

Prisoner psychosis, 79